T5-CCU-646

WHAT OTHERS ARE SAYING...

"*The Other Side of Normal*, by Becki Webb
Becker, gives us a rare and amazing look into the
personal and real world of autism, as it really is.
With current statistics being that autism affects
one in fifty children, it affects us all. Those
of us in the field as professionals, county and
state workers, school teachers, special education teachers, paraprofessionals, police officers,
doctors, nurses, psychologists, and psychiatrists
should be required to read this book as part of
our trainings and licensure processes. From the
professionals to the caregivers, to the person in
the grocery store to the person in the waiting
room, it is a must-read! It reminds us that for
everything we see and think we know, there is a
whole story and real people behind it. What is
our role in this autism? Are we doing our part?
Reading this book gives all of us clarity in how
we can help—the very first step in combatting
this and helping, is understanding."

—Rachael C. Lyons-Herrmann
Director West Metro Learning Connections
Lead Autism Specialist
Special Education Educator:
ASD, MMMI, SLD

"For those of us that know him, Tony has taught us so much about relationships, life, and love. For those who don't, Becki has given him the voice to do just that. This book is one young man's lifetime outlined for all parents, family, friends, and teachers to read and share."

—Lynette Palmsteen, M.Ed

"Becki and I met freshman year at the university. She wrote a weekly column for the university newspaper, and I was her biggest fan. She would share letters and care packages from home, and we would laugh and cry at her sentimental parents. Her parent's unconditional love and support gave her the foundation for her own parenting. Watching Becki and her husband, Dave, raise their three sons has been a remarkable experience. When it comes to her Tony, Becki will stop at nothing to ensure he has the best possible life. It would be impossible to count the hours that Becki has dedicated to autism research, education, and creating awareness. Becki's honest, deeply personal, and sometimes heart-wrenching account is certain to bring clarity, hope, and coping skills to the many parents facing the challenges of raising a child with autism."

—Jody Leigh Jackson
Educator and Curriculum Developer

The OTHER Side OF NORMAL

A look into our NORMAL world with autism

Love,
Tony

Keep the faith!
Becki Becker

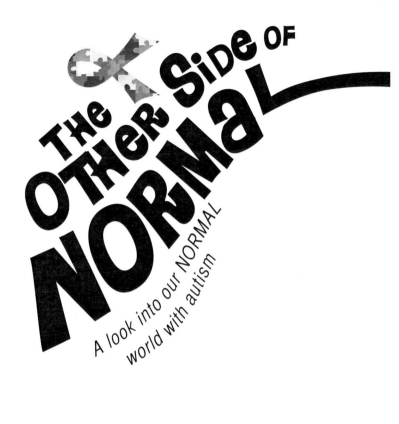

The Other Side of Normal

A look into our NORMAL world with autism

BECKI WEBB BECKER

TATE PUBLISHING
AND ENTERPRISES, LLC

The Other Side of Normal
Copyright © 2013 by Becki Webb Becker. All rights reserved.

No part of this publication may be reproduced, stored in a retrieval system or transmitted in any way by any means, electronic, mechanical, photocopy, recording or otherwise without the prior permission of the author except as provided by USA copyright law.

This book is designed to provide accurate and authoritative information with regard to the subject matter covered. This information is given with the understanding that neither the author nor Tate Publishing, LLC is engaged in rendering legal, professional advice. Since the details of your situation are fact dependent, you should additionally seek the services of a competent professional.

The opinions expressed by the author are not necessarily those of Tate Publishing, LLC.

Published by Tate Publishing & Enterprises, LLC
127 E. Trade Center Terrace | Mustang, Oklahoma 73064 USA
1.888.361.9473 | www.tatepublishing.com

Tate Publishing is committed to excellence in the publishing industry. The company reflects the philosophy established by the founders, based on Psalm 68:11,
"The Lord gave the word and great was the company of those who published it."

Book design copyright © 2013 by Tate Publishing, LLC. All rights reserved.
Cover design by Rodrigo Adolfo
Interior design by Caypeeline Casas

Published in the United States of America

ISBN: 978-1-62746-183-2
1. Family & Relationships / General
2. Family & Relationships / Autism Spectrum Disorders
13.06.05

DeDicaTioN

This book is dedicated to my one and only, Tony,
who made this book come to life just like all
of the make-believe stories he's brought to life
right before our eyes throughout the years.

"We love to use our imagination
because books are a lot of fun!
When you use your imagination, you
can be anywhere and do anything!"
—*Barney & Friends*

According to the US Centers for Disease
Control and Prevention, one out of every fifty
children has an autism spectrum disorder.
These are our real-life encounters of our very
own "one in fifty" as a young adult with autism.

acknowledgments

To my husband, Dave: You've always believed in me and encouraged me to pursue my dream of writing a book. Neither of us had any idea that this would be the path. I thank God every day for our chance meeting all those year ago. I couldn't imagine this journey without you. Your humor brings me out of my stress, and you keep me young. I depend on your strength, and I admire your courage. I love you more than words can say.

To my Michael: You had no idea when you were born just how important your role as a big brother would be. We counted on you more than we should have in your tender young years. But God had a plan for you too, and he blessed us with you. Your sacrifices did not go unnoticed. You are patient and caring and one of the most important people in Tony's life. My love for you is immeasurable.

To my Joey: You were born into chaos, but your purpose was quickly defined. You're our entertainer. Your happy demeanor and joyful noise were welcomed with open arms. We were graced with you in the most difficult time of our marriage. You brought laughter and joy back into our home. Your blessings are abundant, and your kind spirit amazes me every day. Your role as Tony's younger brother isn't an easy one, but it's an important one. You are a true joy.

To my parents, Bill and Carol: You have been our rocks. This family would not exist without your love and support. You've carried us in more ways than we can share. We have always been able to count on you for support in every way, without question. And you've never once made us feel like it's a burden. We know this is tough on you too, and we thank you for never complaining, for adapting, and for always being the first to step up. Your example of faith is what has gotten us through these years.

To my in-laws, Gene and Pat: We thank you for your example of tradition, respect for family, loyalty, and faith. Thank you for always welcoming our chaos into your home and for learning along with us the mysteries of autism. We appreciated the mass dedications and prayers to St. Anthony that you always said on Tony's behalf. Not a day goes by that you aren't missed.

CONTENTS

iNTRODUCTiON

Sometimes, life throws you a curve ball, and it's up to you to decide if you're going to duck or stand strong and face it head-on. Sometimes that's a split-second decision, and other times, it's a lifelong decision. I choose to face it. And every day is a new adventure. My very handsome, supportive husband and I have three uniquely wonderful boys who are currently ages twenty three, twenty, and sixteen. Our twenty-year-old has autism. And these stories will let you into our *normal* world. So sit back, relax, and enjoy the show. It's a simple read, not too stressful and quite entertaining at times. Each chapter is a unique circumstance that we've encountered over the past few years. There is no set order, so read as you like. I hope through our experiences I can shed a new light on autism and what most people perceive it to be. Please keep your sense of humor and an open mind. You may even want to grab a tissue. This is our honest account of situations we've encountered. And I know we are not alone. To those of you new to autism, welcome. I'm excited to have you join us, and you may even learn a little along the way. And to my fellow caretakers, parents, guardians, support staff, and family members reading this that are deep in the trenches teaching, supporting, or raising a child with autism, I commend you. You are facing things that most can't even imagine. You were chosen for this journey, and someone knew you were capable long before you did. You are strong, even if you don't know it yet.

What is Normal anyway?

APRIL 28, 2007

Sometimes, I wonder what it's like to have a normal life. But then again, what is normal anyway? Is there anyone out there who is technically normal? Would anyone even admit to that? In this world today, there are so many families living with exceptions, eccentricities, and abnormalities, if you will. What are your secrets? Everyone has them. What's behind *your* front door? Our story is quite simple. Well, at least we think so.

Let me introduce ourselves: there's Becki (that's me), Dave (loving husband and father), Michael, Tony, and Joey, and a guy named Autism. I say that because we have become so accustomed to this guest in our house—this intruder, this sixth wheel. Unfortunately, I don't believe he's going away anytime soon. He's here, and he's gotten really comfortable with our family. Tony was diagnosed when he was just two years old. I had no idea what was in store for us. I thank God every day for that because if I had known, I don't think I would have been able to cope. And that's the hidden blessing in all of this. It's been a fun, crazy, disheartening, yet wild ride, and we still love every minute of it.

When our Tony, "Toneman" as he's lovingly referred to as, is in movie-mode, we all get to go to the movies for free. Every single day he will pace the kitchen or hallways quoting movies. He usually gets stuck on one movie, and then we all get to see it over and over and over again. It's funny because when my husband and I met, he liked my funny sense of I-should-have-been-a-movie-star mentality. I was always quoting one-liners from movies, mostly from chick flicks, you know, romantic comedies. The difference is that Toneman takes it to the extreme. He won't stop, and it's not just a one-liner; it's an all-nighter and sometimes an all-weeker.

Since Toneman is so Hollywood, we find ourselves thinking this is normal. Doesn't everyone quote a line— no, more like an episode—from *The Magic School Bus* when in science class? Or at the dinner table, doesn't everyone have a child that still finds Barney hilarious in middle school? Doesn't everyone still have to sit through *Dragon Tales* and *Sesame Street* clips played on the family computer? Who knew that YouTube would be so fascinating for kids with autism? They think it's the best thing since popcorn chicken, and french fries! Who knew that blue chips in our house would mean Cool Ranch Doritos—not some financial windfall? Who knew that a simple trip to SuperTarget would be a two-hour analytical trip through their video section? (And trust me, there's not that many to choose from.) Who knew that my three-cornered bathtub would become a snorkeling adventure on a daily basis? Who knew that Toneman's fears would become so intense that he'd be scared to exit the car unless the garage door is closed? Who knew that a simple yawn would cause the Toneman to fly across a room to touch your face with a blessing? (Okay, not the softest blessing. But he does it every single time. Does he know something that we don't or hear something that we can't?) Who knew that he'd call his uncle a World War II fighter pilot when wearing his sleep apnea machine at night? Who knew that my two hundred-pound man-boy would still be scared of the dark? And that he'd come plowing in at any hour of the night to snuggle?

Think about it, how simple is his world? (I said simple, not easy. There's a big difference, which I think you'll get a clearer picture of in later chapters.) It's black and white. There are no social worries. No worries about who likes him or who likes what he's wearing. No worries about who thinks he's cool or who's friends with whom. Toneman doesn't care if his stomach is bulging—he calls himself "Santa Claus" and giggles. He just doesn't care. I realize that he doesn't have those associations or feelings due to our friend, Mr. Autism. But is that a bad thing? Toneman has no financial worries. He may never know the fear of more month at the end of the money (God bless him), or a fear of paying for college, or a fear of saving for retirement. He's very simple, really. He's very matter-of-fact. He is what he is, and he says what he means. Plain and simple. That seems normal, doesn't it? But it's not.

In the movie *Jerry Maguire*, Jerry said, "We live in a cynical world." And we do, with social, financial, and economical pressure. Extreme pressure. But guess what? We put that on ourselves. Did God create this world of autism to show us normal folks (and I use that term lightly) that a person *can* exist without self-doubt, self-pity, self-indulgence, self-everything? Who is normal here, anyway? Who defines that? And could we learn something from all of this? It's interesting. As I sit here, I wonder, how did this happen to our Toneman? Why did it happen to him? What would he be like if he was just *normal*? And then I sit back. Maybe it didn't just happen to him, maybe it happened to us—to all of us—so we could take a step back and realize what's important in life. It's the blue chips, the simplicity of children's videos, the basic need of feeling safe and giving strong hugs and soft kisses when needed—giving someone a sense of security. It's a simpler world, a hidden skill, or a hidden message. We just have to search for it and be open enough to recognize it when it's right in front of us. So for all those families out there living with the exceptions, eccentricities, and abnormalities; who are also asking, "Hey, who signed me up for this *normal* life, anyway?" I know who did. And I thank Him every single day.

i'D Like To
Thank The academy

MARCH 6, 2010

I love Academy Awards night. For those that know me, I'm a huge fan of the movies and everything Hollywood. (Okay, not everything, but I do love the world of make-believe.) I used to imagine myself accepting an Academy Award, and when I played as a child, I was always acting or singing. Maybe it was a foreshadow to what my life would be like raising Tony. To live in our house, you have to speak Hollywood because most of our conversations with Tony revolve around movie quotes. It's quite clever, actually. And remember, Tony is a man of few words. So when he talks, it's very exciting to us. His favorite is old Hollywood, Audrey Hepburn especially. I've had to really study those movies.

So we watched the Academy Awards together this year. He was in my bedroom with pictures of movie stars from his *People* magazines laid out all over the bed. I was in the family room with my glass of wine. At every commercial, I ran upstairs to talk. Well, I talked. He pointed to his list of winners (he kept track) and said, "Okay! You can leave now!" He flipped back and forth between the award show and Turner Classic Movies during commercials. He is an eternal romantic. One time, I ran up to check on Tony, and he was standing up clapping, participating in a standing ovation for Best Actress in a Motion Picture. I was downstairs standing up and clapping too! I just love that night, not because of anything about the award show, but because for a brief moment, Tony and I were speaking the same language.

BeaU BeCKeR ii

MARCH 9, 2010

Beau is a beautiful ivory-colored Lab. We adopted him three years ago after three intense years of working with a behavioral therapist. You see, Tony had such a phobia for dogs that it was truly jeopardizing his quality of life. He wouldn't go outside or even get out of the car until the garage door was shut. For some reason, he had developed this intense fear over the years. He wouldn't walk in the neighborhood, and anytime he ran into a dog, it set him back for months, mentally and behaviorally. It was incredibly stressful on all of us. We avoided dogs at all costs. In fact, the last time I brought him to get his hair cut at a public salon, prior to getting Beau, Tony had a complete horrific meltdown in front of a lobby full of parents and kids, most of which I knew. Unfortunately, someone was outside with a dog on a leash. Perfectly harmless, but a nightmare for my Tony. Pride aside, I proceeded to help him gain his composure so we could exit the hair salon, but he was so scared that he started screaming. There he was, this almost six-foot, two hundred-pound young man, so terrified that he was scaring even the dog. So the therapy started.

His fear had reached a point that the only way out was to face it. Through a small miracle of people, patience, and methodical and intentional conversations about our *someday* dog, Tony started to come around. We talked about our *someday* dog just about every day and posted pictures on the refrigerator. We manifested it. At night, when I'd tuck Tony in, we'd talk about dog names and look at pictures of our old dogs—Beau and Buddy—that my husband and I had when we were first married. We eventually fenced in our backyard so that we'd be ready for a dog, and mostly so that Tony would feel brave enough to go outside again. I can clearly remember the day the fence was finished. I called my husband, literally crying, telling him that Tony was outside, walking the perimeters of the fence and singing a song. A neighbor even called and said, "It's so great to see Tony outside!"

Three years later, after all our hard work, I fell upon a website while researching therapy dogs. Not only was there a five-year waiting list for an autism-trained dog, but they were wildly expensive. I found a breeder a few hours away that had yellow Labradors. They were white-ivory in color, and they were going to be ready in two weeks. It was early February, but we decided to jump in. Now was the time! Over the next two weeks, we prepared Tony for the dog. We bought his kennel, food dishes, dog food, toys, and a leash. We let Tony name him. On the actual day of pick up, Tony was pacing nervously in the kitchen before we left. I said, "Are you ready, Tony?"

And he said, "Sure. Are you ready, Mommy?"

Tears filled my eyes. It was another breakthrough—an actual conversation about a subject that we had worked on for quite a few years. We both took a big breath, and we all got in the car. My youngest son and I actually picked Beau out of the litter. He was the chubbiest and naughtiest one. Loved that! We knew he would be playful yet trainable. And we wanted a big dog, a weighted blanket, so he could someday sleep with Tony in his bed. Beau cried all the way home. Not even a mile down the road, Tony said, "Okay! You can take him back to the farm now!" We all gasped.

"No, Tony. We are his family now. I'm his Mommy, and you are his brother. Beau is going home."

So Tony put on his headphones and kept looking back at Beau, giggling. For the next few weeks, we heard Tony sing, "You're my brother," or "I miss my Mommy," or "You're so naughty, Beau." He'd sing them over and over to the dog. We were all smiling.

Beau grew into a hundred-some-pound Lab just like we wanted. He's been a complete joy to have around. Tony and Beau are inseparable. The dog didn't even know his fate, yet he took to Tony's disability like it was a second nature. He protects Tony, responds to Tony, sits outside Tony's room when he's having a tough time, and barks a special bark when Tony leaves the house. It's like having an extra set of eyes, which is a huge help to all of us. We call Tony and Beau our two toddlers.

And they can get into a lot of trouble together! But it's a very special bond that, even just a few days prior, we didn't think was possible. So I'll put up with all the dog hair, the paw prints, the chewed-up blankets and socks, and additional work it takes to have him because we love our Beau and can't imagine our family without him.

Siblings and Autism

MARCH 11, 2010

I read an article a while ago that focused on siblings. The findings showed that some siblings of autistic preschoolers show signs of developing hyperactivity. It also supports the notion that mothers of young autistic children experience more depression and stress than mothers of typically developing children. (Hmmm... I'll address this at a later time.) The article also states that siblings of children with autism probably should be watched with appropriate academic supports in place. It adds that around 30 percent of siblings have some associated difficulties in behavior, learning, or development.

Well, I'll give you my professional advice on the subject—just some thoughts from a mom who has lived with this subject for many years now. Siblings of a child with autism are a special breed. They are thrown into a world of chaos and unpredictable moments. Every trip to the grocery store, community center, or even restaurant is sometimes humiliating and extremely stressful. Every holiday is an adventure in coping. Every day is a lesson in how to preteach a situation, never being able to rely on spontaneity. They are asked to help watch their autistic sibling so the parents can run errands, or have a conversation, or work from home, or even take a bath. They are asked to not talk loudly, play music, or watch a movie as it might upset their sibling. They are asked to limit visitors to the house to avoid extra chaos. They sacrifice their rooms, clothes, bathrooms, and some- times computers. They watch in horror as a meltdown occurs and try not to add to their parents' stress.

I see these siblings as incredible people. They are exposed to more in their first eighteen years than most adults in a lifetime. They learn to accept people for who they are and not to judge someone if they are differ- ent. They learn to share. They learn that life is not fair. They learn that short-term sacrifices will help achieve long-term goals. They learn to not react to their autistic sibling. Reacting just creates more chaos, more stress. They know that their sibling does not hear their words but only sees their actions, which can make the unwel- comed behavior continue. Siblings have been known to change their diets to accommodate the family. Siblings give up a Saturday night with friends so their parents can get a much-needed break. I don't doubt that the above findings are true. I'm sure they will find a lot of long-term effects on these siblings. I just wish some of the studies would also find the incredible, undeni- able, God-given coping skills that these kids develop. They are the true heroes of autism.

SUPPORT GROUPS

APRIL 2, 2010

There are a few support groups that I crave. And they're not the typical ones. They're my friends, and they don't even realize just how much I lean on them. Aside from my husband and my parents, they are the ones who I can go to when I need to talk, or when I need to just have fun and leave the stress behind. Whether it's daily calls, coffee, lunch, e-mail, Facebook chats, or bonfires with the neighbors, my friends seem to know just what I need for support. They are always ready to listen, always there to be a sounding board, always giving me positive feedback on how I'm doing. I don't know how I'd survive without them. They surround me with heartwarming reinforcement and sometimes just sit and listen. And when my stress bucket is full, they know to not ask and to just help me smile and laugh. There are no questions asked when the noise level fills the background when I'm on the phone, or the noise seeps out the windows. No questions when we are frantically looking for our wanderer, no questions when they see us drive by from yet another car ride for the day, no questions when my dark circles have decided to move in for the winter, and no questions when I seem to forget what we were just talking about. A friend once gave me a card that read, "You're the kind of person this world needs more of because you live what you believe in and reach out to make a difference."

I work on that daily. As a parent of a special needs child, I want to acknowledge all of our supportive friends for helping me stay strong, focused, and determined. To you all, I send a sincere, heartfelt hug for all you do, even if you don't know you're doing it.

a BReakThROUgh DaY

APRIL 7, 2010

Tony had a breakthrough when he was seventeen. Not sure why or how, but one day, he just decided to start using the telephone. He'd spent the prior two days reading the new local telephone book (page by page, like it was a novel) as he usually does when we get our new phone books. (Seriously, he actually reads it.) Then mysteriously one Friday morning, he called one of my girlfriends to ask for a video twice and even had her deliver it while I was gone, which she did. How cute was that? Then he called 911, which ended up being a great teaching moment. The girl on the phone was so nice and asked him questions, which he didn't answer, and then asked him to give his mom the phone, and he did. She told me she made a note of his name and disability and said we could call the nonemergency number anytime to practice. She said he did a great job of listening. Wow, that could have turned out much differently! *Then* he called my other neighbor and asked if her new puppy, Maggy, could come over and play. *Then* he called Grandma and talked about Easter for over ten minutes! She was thrilled! *Then* he called his big brother, who's away at college, and asked when he'd be home and actually had a nice conversation! *Then* he called yet another neighbor and asked about her trip to Mexico. *Then*, a few hours later, he ordered himself a gluten-free pizza and had it delivered. I had to do my own investigating and found out who he called by using the redial button on our landline phone (yes, we still have one). He did this all from his bedroom while reading a magazine and watching a movie.

What? Oh my goodness! Did that just happen? Tony had a huge smile on his face all day long. I was so proud of him! He's never used the phone before and has never been able to carry on a conversation. We assumed it was because he couldn't visually see the other person on the phone. He even went so far as to hide all of our phones because he doesn't like the sound of the ring. Wow, his world has really opened up. So yes, now there's another thing to monitor, but more importantly, a major breakthrough!

LeT iT Be

APRIL 12, 2010

One of my all-time favorite songs is "Let it Be," by the Beatles. Tony and I were on one of our field trips riding in my car with the top down, and he turned up the radio. This song was playing. He sang it to me—word for word, perfect pitch—while rocking softly back and forth. It was the most glorious moment between a mom and her not-so-verbal son. His language was clear, and he added vibrato—and he knows I love it when he does that. He has such a beautiful voice. And as I was driving, wiping the tears from my eyes, he grabbed my hand and kissed it, as if to say, "It will all be okay." These are the moments I treasure. Just the two of us on our daily drive in our convertible. There's something about the wind in his face—it's such wonderful therapy for him. I'm sure it's fulfilling his sensory needs, but I find it fulfilling mine too. It's very euphoric. Take a minute and listen to the lyrics of this song as if it was talking about the mystery of autism.

It really takes on a new dimension. We are all hoping that these kids will not only *see* someday, but that there will be an answer in their lifetime.

a COUPLe Of Rough weeks

APRIL 25, 2010

It's inevitable. More often than not, we have a couple of rough weeks. Seems to be around a full moon, so I have to admit, we do watch the moon cycles. There comes a time when the major meltdowns take over. His anxiety climbs to a point where he bursts. He will run outside screaming, swearing, slamming doors, breaking things; none of us know how to help him. It's so frustrating and so mentally exhausting. He seems like he wants to climb out of his skin. He can't tell us how he feels, so we have to play these guessing games. He's trying to run from us and just can't seem to settle himself down. He's immediately remorseful and sincere when he tells us he's "so, so sorry."

But then he turns around and does it again a few seconds later. Even Beau doesn't know what to do. Sometimes I just want to hide. Sometimes I just want to pout and scream myself. It stops me in my tracks and puts me in a state where I just can't seem to focus. Where did my child go? Who is this? It's very sad and humbling to admit this, but I do mourn the loss of my son on a daily basis. I do. And I'm reminded daily of just how different his life is from what I had imagined for him. Is this the lesson I'm supposed to learn?

FiELD TRiPS

MAY 11, 2010

Every spring is a tough transition for Tony. When May arrives, we count down the days until summer vacation. Well, Tony does. I panic a little as I need to get some things on the schedule to keep Tony's routine steady. He'll be in summer school, but that's just a couple of hours per day. I look for affordable things. There are many wonderful camps for kids with autism, but between you and me, they are outrageously priced. I'm sure it costs a ton to hire staff that is one to one with clients.

Tony's entertainment has been to go on daily field trips, which are car rides. We have been hitting just about every little city in the southwest suburbs. He loves the old buildings, the small towns, the country fields, and the hills. And I must say, I've discovered a lot too. I've never really been able to venture out and just go for a drive. Our schedule was always so routine; there was no deviation allowed. Is this a sign that Tony's becoming more independent? Or that he wants to explore the world around him more? Or is it related to the fact that he's memorized the map that Grandpa gave him? Is he studying the roads? Counting miles or mile markers? I remember clearly one weekend, we were driving home to my parents' house. My husband took a different way (I think there was construction), and Tony had a meltdown for two hours. It was an extremely stressful drive. I think he was around five or six years old. Now we have learned that everything is pre-planned, pre-taught. We warn Tony of all construction and all unexpected stops. It's become natural for us to do that.

Sometimes, I look at my siblings' families and notice just how flexible everyone is. I noticed that they can change plans at the last minute or that they can actually take three hours to make a plan. Everyone's okay with that, and everyone's on board when a decision is finally made. Not so in our house. We could never do that. I don't mean to sound negative. I just wanted to point out how everyone in the house has adapted to this disorder. And why are we adapting? Why can't we just fix it? Why can't we just discipline him like we could our other two sons? Those are million-dollar questions. These things that we've learned are so much deeper than just simply a discipline problem. It's a neurological disorder. It's frustrating. It's maddening. And I'm just one of millions of moms and dads out there who are dealing with the same things—day in and day out. We don't have meetings about it, and we don't talk about it. We've all just adapted. Why? To avoid a meltdown. To avoid stress. To avoid pain. I think I was better at pushing him when he was younger. These teenage years are tough regardless if a child has a disability or not, right? Hormones and autism, not a pretty sight. I'm just sayin'.

MY TYPiCaL DaY

MAY 12, 2010

Here is a short story that my husband wrote years ago through the eyes of Tony, about the same time my husband had to make an unexpected career change. This story made me chuckle and brought back lots of memories. It's interesting to read this from my husband's account. He used to leave for work at 4:00 a.m. or 5:00 a.m. so he was not around in the mornings, and an early bedtime was right in sync with Tony's bedtime. It also seemed at the time that our life revolved around their favorite Mexican restaurant. We used it as a reward for good behavior or sometimes as a treat for everyone.

My Typical Day
Tony Becker

Hi, my name is Tony. I'd like to walk you through a typical day of my quirky family. It all starts with my mom and dad shutting their loud radio off every morning about four to five times. Then they finally get out of *my* bed—the one that they started sleeping in and I took over. Mom starts out in the shower while I pull and poke at my dad's arms and all that loose skin on his elbow. He seems to get irritated, but I figure if he doesn't like it, then he can get out of *my* bed. Anyway, I turn on the TV and start to watch *Magic School Bus*. Dad always tells me to turn it down, but I know he really likes it because I always see him watching my videos over my shoulder, which is not permitted in my house.

Then it's finally time for me to get in the shower. I take a twenty-minute shower, which is pretty cool because there was a time when I couldn't stand to have water poured over my head. I would completely freak out, and my dad would become a basket case. I like to sing in the shower because I have a fabulous voice, and no one else is allowed to sing in this house because they have such bad voices, except my mom. She's pretty good. When I'm done with my shower, I go singing through the house just to wake up everybody. I make such a good alarm clock. I sing for my older brother and pounce on my younger brother to wake him up. I then go down to the kitchen to get on Mom's computer, which is incredibly slow. Mom gives me my vitamins, and I outthink the computer—all while the rest of the people are getting up.

Dad tries to sneak down into the kitchen, but I don't allow him in because he hasn't been around for the first thirteen years of my mornings, so why is he now trying to get into my morning inner circle? Mom pours me a baggie of cereal, and we head off to school. Before I fill you in about my school day, let me tell you about my brothers. These guys are my two best friends. My older brother is like another parent. He's so kind but can discipline with the best of them. "I'm going to call Dad!" he threatens while I scream at a hundred decibels, "*No!*" One minute I will be wrestling him, and the next he's cooking me a pizza. He's always making sure I'm safe. You know, I can get into a lot of stuff. He is one of my two best friends.

Now, let me tell you about the other one. He's younger than me, and he is still here. I don't know why he hasn't left yet. For so long, it was just my older brother and me, but then Mom's stomach got big, and now there is another person in this house. My younger brother does things to annoy me, like be in the same room as me, yawn, and stretch. He is always there though when it's time for bed. I lie in the same bed as Joey and my dad until they fall asleep, then I go back in to *my* bed with Mom. I'm pretty sneaky.

Getting back to school, Mom drops me off at the curb, and I slowly walk in, only to find a chunk of snow to pick up and eat. My classes are pretty easy, and I do like some of them, but there are others that I could do without. But enough about school. I get home and get right on that slow computer again. This time I've got one movie running in eight different frames with the scenes two seconds apart; my dad is amazed, and the computer has gotten slower yet. I slam my fist down on the table and scream, "God—" Then my mom stops me, and I finish with "Bless the Lord, Amen!"

It all works out after all, and I'm back to it. I begin to think I'm hungry, so I go to the cupboard and get some chips and salsa. After I finish the first bowl of salsa, I ask, "What's for dinner?"

I would think that by the looks of it, these other people in the house aren't really doing anything, so why not cook me dinner? Dad asks me what I'm hungry for, and I always answer, "How about [insert Mexican restaurant here]?"

Dad tells me no again, but I can't understand why, so I start to scream. "Where's Mommy?" Dad tells me that she's at an appointment. "Where's Mommy?" Dad tells me again she's at an appointment. Apparently, this guy doesn't get it. "Where's Mommy?"

"*She's at an appointment!*" my older brother yells.

Now is a good time to hit younger brother. He just yawned. So off to the Mexican restaurant we go. Older brother orders me the same thing that I always get. "He'll have the chicken strips with the alphabet tater tots, and could you bring some more chips and two more salsas, please? He goes through them fast."

After I finish five cups of salsa and three baskets of chips, I figure I'm not really hungry tonight. "A big box," I tell the person that keeps coming with the chips.

I fill the box with chips and salsa and the rest of my chicken and alphabet tater tots. It's time to go home now, but wait, I need to go to the bathroom, and once again my big brother takes me. So we're on our way home because it's time to go to bed, and bedtime is at nine at the latest. "Hey, you!" I say to my younger brother. "Time for bed. Daddy, lie down."

After the day is done, I think I've got a pretty nice life. Thanks, Mom, Dad, older brother, and younger brother. I really do love you.

So there you have it. A glimpse of a typical day written by someone other than Mom. Granted, this was quite a few years ago, and our eating habits have changed for the better. It's interesting to read the familiar chaos and remember the demands of that time. All with one purpose: to create peace in our home on a daily basis. Interestingly enough, it brings a smile to my face as I read this today knowing just how far we've actually come.

Riding in the Car with Tony

MAY 27, 2010

Yes, we're still going on our field trips. Thank goodness gas prices are dropping. We go on two, maybe three rides a day when the weather is nice. Who would have known that this car purchase was going to be such a wonderful sensory activity for Tony? Tony uses his trusty road atlas and he picks a direction in which to travel every day. (I've limited him to a small radius.) I love that he's becoming so aware of his surroundings and that he wants to explore. We've pretty much hit all the western suburbs in the area. We have a route that takes us to a very popular lake in the area, and he loves watching the boats and seeing the sparkle on the water, and so do I. We don't get out of the car; we just drive with the top down. We get our daily dose of vitamin D and of classic '70s and '80s music. He sings, he rocks, and he dances with his hands up in the air. He's completely euphoric. I have to say that it's been a great therapy for me too. It's really hard to make time for a ride. I mean, I do need to work. There are appointments to make, training, and presentations to do; there's laundry, the house to clean, groceries to buy, errands to run, calls to return, bills to pay, yada, yada, yada.

However, in his world, this is a necessity. It's something he looks forward to every day. It's time alone, just he and I, and it's time spent out in the world. What am I to learn from this? I guess I'm learning to just let it be. Taking the time to enjoy this beautiful state we live in. Taking the time to slow down and smell the lilacs. Slow down to see the farmers' markets. Slow down and watch the boats on the lake. Slow down and see the sunset out to the west. Slow down and watch the storms approach. Have I gotten so busy and overwhelmed with life that this seems stressful? I guess I have. I'm really glad Tony is slowing me down.

THings THaT Make Me Happy

MAY 28, 2010

Overflowing bubble bath
Beau as my pillow
Bonfires
Lazy Beau
Rolling around on the grass
with Mom's comforter
My brothers

This is Tony's list of things that make him happy. It's so simple, yet so complicated.

ONE STEP FORWARD, TWO STEPS BACK

JUNE 25, 2010

I have started writing this piece for over two weeks now. Summer has begun, and everything has changed. It was a very tough transition for everyone. Tony was doing fantastic toward the end of the school year. We were all holding our breath and really thought that he'd end the year on a positive note. He attended my niece's graduation party down at my parents' house and had a fantastic weekend. We were so proud of him! He was very social, alert, aware, and conversational. It was a huge step forward; we were thrilled. It was a great weekend.

However, when we got back home and back to school, it was another story. He only had four days of school left, and I kept wondering if we should just be done. But every day was good, so we kept going— until that last day. It was horrible. Let's just say that it involved the crisis team, and unfortunately, his special ed teacher took the brunt of his anger. Not the way I wanted it to end. I felt horrible, and Tony was so remorseful. Although the remorse is a good thing, the temper is a very bad thing that even Tony can't control when his anxiety level is peaked. That is the challenge we face daily.

So school ended, and the summer began. I've had to make certain that he has a schedule to follow and things to do. To aid this, I hired my niece to come over two days a week. It's been the best decision we ever made! She is so good with Tony. He loves having her around. It's like he has a friend over to hang with, a peer. It's so fun watching them talk, plan their day, and make homemade salsa after a trip to the farmers' market. She works as a paraprofessional during the school year, so she has a lot of experience with autism. Plus, they grew up together. She's always been one of Tony's favorites, and she's always had a special way with him. She's fearless with him, and we love that. It not only gives me a break, but it allows me to have time alone with my other sons. And time to work from home. Autism or not, bills still have to be paid, right?

The stress has been intense for my husband and I, his younger brother, and yes, even Tony. He's missing his older brother, who is living in his college town, and like all things in life, it's a constant adjustment. See, that's the difference between an autistic brain and our brain. They can't adjust. It's something we all take for granted. But for someone with autism, it's something that has to be taught and learned and can take a lifetime to conquer.

STORMS

JUNE 28, 2010

I was so proud of Tony last weekend! My parents' house was hit by a tornado last Friday night, and we spent the weekend helping them clean up the damage. We had to drive back and forth both days—that's about an hour and a half each direction. We spent hours in the heat and humidity cleaning up the mess. Because of this, they still don't have electricity, which means no TV, no videos or movies, and no air-conditioning. And for Tony, this means *change*. Change is hard for anyone. Change for someone with autism is *extremely* hard because it's unknown or unexpected, or better yet, unpredictable. And that causes stress. Stress causes meltdowns. Meltdowns can cause damage, and the pattern continues.

Tony stayed occupied by hanging out in the basement with a flashlight looking at old pictures and reading old books. There was a lot of chaos. A lot of people coming and going, and a lot of noise from the generator and the tree chipper. I was a little worried but needed to be there to help out and to make sure my parents were coping with all of their *change*. It's so hard to see big old trees flattened by storms. Over sixteen beautiful trees, trees with history, my dad brought back from the northern part of the state back in the late '70s—birch, northern pine, etc.—and we've watched them grow through the years. The good news is that no one was hurt from this *change*. The house was left untouched, except for some shingles and a twisted antenna. The house, I'm sure, was protected by prayer. Lots and lots of prayer. Tony even got on the phone to talk to his aunt to tell her about it and confirm a visit to their house—he's been begging to go see them. And remember, this is a new skill for him! I was very proud of him to handle all the chaos and the incredible change it's going to be every time we go down to Grandma and Grandpa's house. I documented the storm damage in a book so he can see the changes—before and after—to help him process this permanent change on how Grandma and Grandpa's house looks now. Maybe I should make one for the rest of us too. We could all use a little help coping.

Yesterday's Field Trip

JUNE 29, 2010

Yesterday, my youngest son and I got brave and took Tony to a large-chain discount store. It has been quite a long time since we've taken him there on our own. I seem to remember a time when he had an incredibly loud meltdown in the middle of that particular store. It's a vague memory. If I haven't mentioned it before, I'll mention it now; I have a gift of blocking out stressful memories—or maybe not blocking them out, but filing them away because my stress bucket gets full. I like to think of it as a gift because I'd be walking a fine line if I held on to all that stress. I'm not a huge fan of this store, mostly because of their business practices and because of the harmful ingredients they market for their own line of products. But you can't deny their low prices on old movies, gluten-free dry goods, and adult shoes with Velcro—which are extremely hard to find, trust me. We had talked about the field trip on one of our long car rides last weekend. I asked if he wanted to go look for shoes since Beau chewed on his sandals and his shoes (much provoked by Tony, I'm sure). So this morning, he came into my office and said very quietly, "Store today? New shoes? I like headphones." In other words, he means he could wear headphones to block out unpredictable noises.

I couldn't say no. He was using his manners, asking appropriate questions, and actually problem-solving all at once. Another breakthrough! Thank goodness for the headphones because as we pulled up, we saw major construction at this particular store. (Heaven, help me.) We got out and chased after Tony as he ran excitedly into the store. We found the shoes, and he got a five-dollar movie—Audrey Hepburn's *Breakfast at Tiffany's*, his favorite classic. I couldn't resist. Then he asked, "Treat for Beau?" Again, he had me at his mercy. I was so excited for the conversation—broken English or not. As we left the store, he said, "Good-bye, friend!" to the greeter.

She smiled, obviously understanding our situation, as Tony had not one, but two headphones on: one small pair from his DVD player, and another big noise–canceling headphone for school. I had to laugh. I didn't see that as he got out of the car. He came very prepared! I asked my younger son if anyone stared at us or if he was uncomfortable at all. He said he didn't care if anyone stared; he loves his brother. He said if anyone had stared or made a comment, he would just say, "Hey! My brother has autism. What's your problem?"

I decided that wasn't very polite—especially for a thirteen-year-old. So I gave him some better words to use next time: "Hey, my brother has autism. Do you have any questions?" (just in case he ever needs them). He was okay with that. Another teachable moment for all of us.

DOES HE RULE THE HOUSE?

JULY 8, 2010

I overheard a comment from a family member last weekend. He commented that Tony ruled the house and that we all tiptoed around him. It made me sad, but it's so true. I didn't realize how evident that was until last weekend. It's so *normal* for us that we don't even notice it anymore. But last weekend, we were staying at my parents' house, and it really became apparent. Tony has certain rules that we've all just become accustomed to. We've all adjusted because he can't. It's not easy, and it makes for a very tense environment sometimes. Keep in mind there is no explanation for any of these. They just are.

Here's what I noticed:

> Rule #1: Do not yawn. Especially yawning *and* making any kind of noise at the same time.

59

Rule #2: Do not have loud background noise. That means TVs, radios, computers, vacuums, or hand mixers (can use, but need to alert him first).

Rule #3: Do not sneeze and scream at the same time (some people do that without realizing it).

Rule #4: Do not say "Blah, blah, blah" while speaking.

Rule #5: I need to see all your old photographs and yearbooks when I visit.

Rule #6: I also need to take a mental inventory of all your DVDs and any VHS movies you may have.

Rule #7: I rule the TV. I will block the other channels while I'm here but will unblock them before I go, if I remember.

Rule #8: No loud, unexpected laughter. Please.

Rule #9: Unlimited baths are expected.

Rule #10: Friday night is pizza night. It must be gluten-free.

Rule #11: I need to touch you on the chin and the head every time you yawn, sneeze, or sing.

Rule #12: Keep things orderly and predictable. Please. I need to know the schedule.

Rule #13: No deviations in the schedule. Please.

Rule #14: Absolutely do not change your mind or give me more options.

Rule #15: No whistling.

There are so many other things I could add. So many that they don't even seem odd to me anymore. To all those we've visited, I'm sorry. I hope it doesn't reflect as bad parenting. It is what it is. It's part of his disorder, part of his *dis*-ease. Some of these rules come and go; some have been around for years. What is the lesson here? I'd appreciate any and all advice. In the meantime, we will continue to follow the rules because they keep peace in our house. And peace of mind is all we're asking for.

Heavy is the Load,
but Mighty are the
Supporters

AUGUST 5, 2010

Summer is a wonderful time, and I truly believe that people who live in the Midwest pump as much as they can into their summer days. We get three or four months of nice, warm weather to enjoy, and then the cold comes into play. We continue our daily rides, burning through the gas, and there have been a few days that we've almost gotten caught in the rain; nothing makes Tony laugh harder than when it starts to rain, and we have to pull over to put the top up. With that said, the rides at dusk have been absolutely gorgeous. It's become as much of a therapy session for us as it is for Tony.

Last weekend, I was able to get away alone for some much-needed *therapy*. Every summer a large group of my college friends get together at a resort in the northern part of the state. We call ourselves GOOF, which simply stands for Group Of Our Friends. I don't make it every year, and on rare occasions, both my husband and I get to go. But this time, I really needed a break. My husband could tell, so he sent me alone. Before I left, I posted this on my Facebook page: "College reunion this weekend! Some things just get better with time... Love to slip back in time and 'forget about life for a while.' Can't wait to see everyone again!"

Well, I wasn't disappointed. I had an incredible time, even lost my voice from all the talking and laughing. Everything at home went well, and my hubby did a wonderful job. I didn't even have to check in, except for the texts I sent because I somehow missed the chaos. It was truly a mental break for me. A lot of my old friends will read this, so I want to take this moment to thank all of them for allowing me to relax. We didn't talk much about autism or therapies or stress or hard times. We just reminisced, talked, and laughed until we couldn't breathe, remembering how things were at college in the '80s.

One friend came in all the way from Hong Kong, and we even had one from Florida. We hadn't seen her in twenty years, but the minute we did, it was as if no time had passed at all. There was a lot of love and joy in the room as we reconnected with those who had a part in forming who we became. We've all aged, but when we get together, that doesn't matter. We look at each other and see an old friend. These people helped me that weekend more than they'll ever know. For a few short days, I was just *me*. I wasn't someone's mom or even Tony's mom, or the autism writer, or the business builder; I was just me. And it was really nice to get to know me again.

"Some people come into our lives and quickly go. Others stay a while, make footprints on our hearts, and we are never, ever the same" (Unknown).

Here's to you—all of you GOOFers! Thanks again for the belly laughs. See you next year.

HELLO, TWELFTH GRADE

SEPTEMBER 13, 2010

Tony and I have had a ritual for the past twelve years. Every August, we start preparing for the first day of school. When Tony was six—and not quite verbal—we started reading a book called *Hello First Grade,* by Joanne Ryder. It told a story of a little boy moving on to first grade and all the new adventures he'd encounter. For some reason, it stuck; and every year toward the end of summer, we start saying, "Hello, second grade!" then "Hello, third grade!" You get the idea. This year was no exception. Tony said, "Hello, twelfth grade!" Then he smiled. "Next year, hello, college?" My heart ached. We've had this conversation before.

Three years ago, while touring a college with his older brother, Tony announced in the car, "Tony college September 2011!" Everyone in the car gasped. We had never even considered that he understood what the next step would be. We all looked at each other with sadness and a realization that he would never know that reality. So ever since, we talk about Tony's college being in his hometown, and he can live with Mom and Dad. He seems okay with that for now.

So far, school is going good. He has a shortened day, and it seems to be a good fit. My niece works as his personal care attendant (PCA) and still comes to hang with Tony weekly. They had a great summer together. As I mentioned, my niece is fearless, and we really love that about her. She takes him everywhere: swimming, pet stores, thrift stores, the library, shopping malls, restaurants, Grandma and Grandpa's house, farmers' markets, apple farms, and even flower gardens. He's good for her, and I'm sure because he sees her as his peer. Believe it or not, I do think he gets that it's not cool to constantly hang with your mom when you're in high school. And that's great! That's kind of *normal*. Hopefully, we've turned the corner on puberty, hormones, and mood swings. One can only hope.

As I reflect on Tony's years through the school system, I often wonder if we have even tapped into his knowledge potential. And it's no one's fault. He wouldn't let us in. He just doesn't learn the way others do. I believe he's like a computer, and we have to find the backdoor approach to see what really lies behind that main screen. Maybe then we can finally speak the same language, and he can introduce me to his world.

aUTiSM aND
The GF DieT

SEPTEMBER 16, 2010

I found an article from Dr. Mercola a few years ago called "The Toxic Origins of Autism" (http://articles. mercola.com). I've read it quite a few times, and it states three main factors or origins for autism:

1. *Autoimmune disease.* Parents of autistic children, particularly mothers, tend to have a greater rate of autoimmune diseases. Things like food allergies, chronic fatigue syndrome, fibromyalgia, and other more subtle symptoms.

2. *Gene mutations.* Children with autism tend to have more gene expressions that are inefficient for detoxification. These so-called mutations tend to be unpredictable, and every autistic

child's set is slightly different, along with their own unique expression of autism.

3. *Chronic infections.* Chronic infections like Lyme disease are extremely common in autistic children and may even be causing the gene mutations. Typically, the child gets the disease not from a tick bite, but from their mother who may be a silent carrier of the illness. Ironically, the major symptom of Lyme disease in a child is not autism but rather hyperactivity, learning disorders, depression, early puberty, and slight delays in motor development. The symptoms can actually stay silent or nearly silent for up to twenty years. It goes on to state that the diet should be tailored, avoiding pasteurized milk, MSG, high-fructose corn syrup—basically all processed food.

This got me thinking over and over again that we should give the gluten-free diet another try. We had tried it when Tony was four years old. My youngest son was a newborn then, and I wanted to try this new diet everyone was talking about on the autism chat rooms and in the research on the autism sites.

That was thirteen years ago. We had to shop at a co-op about forty-five minutes away. There were no prepackaged products, and you had to use types of flour I've never even heard of and many unusual ingredients. It was just too much to take on with a two-month-old, a four-year-old with autism, and a six-and-a-half-year-old. At the time, I have to admit, I was already overwhelmed. However, I've always kept it in the back of my mind and have always thought that someday, we would master this way of eating—all of us.

Fast-forward to November of 2009, Elisabeth Hasselbeck is on *The View*, talking about her new book *The G-Free Diet: A Gluten-Free Survival Guide*. She has celiac disease and has to eat only gluten-free (GF) foods. She said her book was an easy way to get started—a beginner's guide. Soon after, a very dear friend from college mailed me the book, knowing that I had wanted to learn more. I read it in two days, and after a very bad episode at school and at home (one of Tony's meltdowns), we decided to start the very next day. I told my husband that I would take it meal by meal so that I wouldn't feel overwhelmed. We'd just take it slow and learn as we go. Well, that was three days before Thanksgiving of 2009.

Today, I'm very proud to report that Tony is completely gluten-free, and other than sneaking a few chocolate chip cookies now and then, he has not deviated one bit. (He later paid dearly for that choice—major stomach pains—and I'm sure he learned his lesson.) Here's the best part: Tony lost thirty pounds! He looks fantastic, and I know he feels fantastic. He's never fought me on this—he's adapted. He'll even go so far as to tell me, "Nope! Can't eat that, not gluten-free!" when I try to introduce a new food. But once we say it *is* gluten-free, he usually eats the new food.

His irritable bowel syndrome (IBS) symptoms are gone. His behavior has improved. His sleeping patterns are better. And his complexion is better. I couldn't

believe how much GF food is available at our local grocery store. It's become a very popular way of eating, and
even local restaurants are offering GF options. He still
has pizza night; we found a great local pizza place that
delivers GF pizza. He can still have chips and salsa. We
just stopped all the processed junk food. And yes, there
was a definite detoxification period thrown in with
the holidays, which were crazy enough that we barely
noticed. (Okay, we did notice, but we got through it.)

Was it the best time to cut out all convenient foods?
No. But is there ever a best time? You must realize that
gluten (a wheat protein) is in just about everything
we eat in today's society. When was the last time we
ate only things with ingredients we could pronounce?
Without realizing it, we had let the food manufactur-
ers dictate what we eat. And we've become literally
addicted to their foods, again without realizing it. Now
I know there's a definite connection here between the
food we eat and disease. Nutrition has a direct impact
on a child's development. And a growing body of evi-
dence suggests that eliminating gluten from the diet
can have a beneficial effect on children diagnosed with
autism. One of the biggest "aha" moments from that
book went something like this: however inconvenient
the gluten-free diets might seem, however much resist-
ance you might meet at your child's school or even in
the pediatrician's office, isn't it worth a try? Truthfully, a
new diet isn't hard. It's the autism that's hard.

GRANDPA GENE

OCTOBER 11, 2010

I've often wondered how Tony would take a death in the family. Before my father-in-law passed away, we had watched him suffer for years, and we were all prepared, or so we thought. He had been getting progressively worse. We talked about what we'd do with Tony in this situation. We wanted desperately for him to be able to say good-bye to Grandpa. We took Tony to the hospital the night before he died. We were nervous as we hadn't ever brought Tony to the hospital. Lots of things ripped through our minds. The fluorescent lighting (the humming makes him scream), the unpredictable noises from other people, the elevators, the smells, the cords and equipment, the beeping equipment, the computer screens, the how-would-we-escape-if-he-started-to-scream fear—we thought of it all in a matter of a few seconds. That's a gift, so to speak, that a parent acquires while raising a child with autism. I call it crisis management with a twist—you never get to manage a crisis the same way twice. Every situation is a mystery to unravel, to try to solve, to try to cope.

However, on that peaceful night, Tony amazed us. He walked through the hospital effortlessly. When we got to Grandpa's room, it was full of people, which normally would have been hard for him. Tony sat down by his big brother. That alone usually upsets him. Not the fact that he saw his older brother—he adores him—but the fact that his older brother comes and goes. He no longer gets to see him every day, so the "change" is always a hard adjustment. But not that night; Tony held Grandpa's hand, leaned in very close, and stared. He whispered something so sweet, so soft, that it made me sob. He said, "I'll miss you, and I'll see you again in heaven someday."

Even today, when I think back, I'm still amazed. I'm amazed that he understood. I'm amazed that he remained calm. And I'm really amazed that he talked directly to Grandpa Gene. Scripted or not, he talked directly to him. I shouldn't be so surprised. I mean, he *has* read the Bible, and he loves to read biographies and life stories. He knows our genealogy better than anyone else in the extended family. He can probably process death better than all of us.

The very next evening, Grandpa Gene passed away. We were so happy that everyone got to say good-bye. We talked to Tony in great lengths about the process of the funeral, and we decided to have a private viewing for Tony. Again, he amazed us. He was silent, he knelt and prayed, and he kissed Grandpa and made the sign of the cross on his forehead. I took some pictures from afar for him to process it more, and we made a scrapbook. Through this whole process, we couldn't have gotten through it all without the help of my mom. She literally dropped everything and came to stay with us for an entire week so I could be by my husband's side in making the funeral preparations and helping his family with all the details. I truly don't know what we would have done without her. Someone had to stay back with Tony, and she didn't hesitate for a minute to come to our rescue. That says a lot about her character. She's the kind of person I aspire to be. So thank you, Mom.

I'm also grateful for my sister-in-law who came to stay with Tony so my mom could attend the funeral. She is an occupational therapist, and she came armed with activities. Tony also adores her. They ended up taking a lot of pictures in the backyard—pictures of Tony posing with our dog Beau, that we can use for his graduation.

Funerals seem to bring out the very best in people. We were amazed by those who took time to come or send a card or even an e-mail. Every one of them touched our hearts. But Tony touched our hearts the most. It gave my husband and me a glimpse into his mind. To know that he actually understands death is still humbling to me. To know that he knew enough to say good-bye, to know that he will forever memorize the sight of Grandpa's face and his dash. The dash of his life, the dash that now defines his life. I know Grandpa Gene's legacy will live on. Tony will make sure of that.

In loving memory of Grandpa Gene,
September 26, 1928 - *dash* - September 21, 2010.

TONY'S PRAYER

OCTOBER 26, 2010

I found an old bookmark that my oldest son made in grade school years ago for Grandparents' Day. It's now next to Tony's bed, and he reads it nightly:

**There's a Special Place in
Heaven for Grandparents**

**Few can bring the warmth we can find in
their embrace, and little more is needed to
bring love than the smile on their face.**

**They've a supply of precious stories, yet
they've time to wipe a tear or give us reasons
to make us laugh; they grow more precious
through the years.**

**I believe that God sent us grandparents as
our legacy from above, to share the moments
of our life as extra measures of love.**

—unknown author

I can see that Tony is still processing his grandpa's death. It warms my heart to know that he is learning these coping skills and that he is thinking about his grandpa Gene. You see, prayer is not tangible. You cannot see it. You have to think it. And children with autism have a very hard time processing things that are not tangible. That was a huge step! It's another life skill to add to the list, one that most of us simply take for granted.

The chRiSTMaS LiST

OCTOBER 27, 2010

This is not a typical Christmas wish list for your average seventeen-year-old. But then again, we aren't looking for typical. We are just thrilled that he sat down on his own and made his wish list. These are things that will make him happy—things he can memorize study, dissect, and explore. Just some simple DVDs and books to add to his collection, and then all will be good in his world.

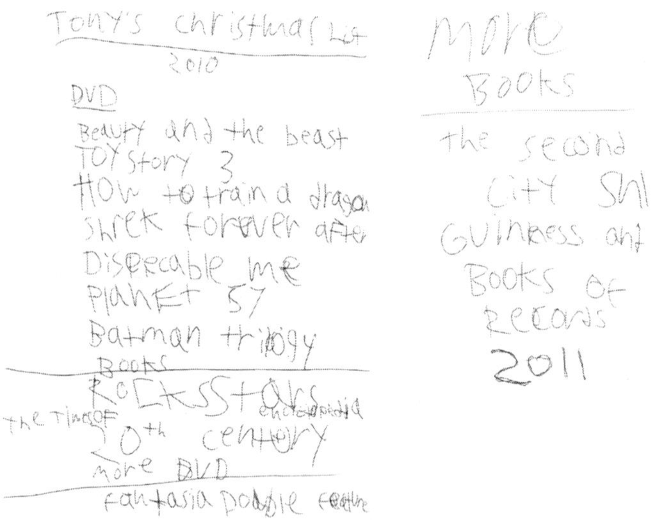

[Handwritten note:]

Tony's christmas List
2010

DVD
Beauty and the beast
Toy Story 3
How to train a dragon
Shrek forever after
Despicable me
Planet 57
Batman trilogy
Books
Rock Stars Encyclopedia
The Times of 20th century
More DVD
Fantasia double feature

More Books
the second city SNL
Guinness ant Books of Records
2011

DVDs: *Beauty and the Beast, Toy Story 3, How to Train Your Dragon, Shrek Forever After, Despicable Me, Planet 57, Batman* trilogy.

Books: Rock Stars Encyclopedia, *The Times of the 20th Century.*

More DVDs: *Fantasia Double Feature.*

More Books: *The Second City SNL (Saturday Night Live), Guinness Book of World Records 2011.*

At least there's plenty on the list for his birthday too!

aNOTheR TURNiNg POiNT

NOVEMBER 23, 2010

For years, a certain song has been sort of an anthem for me. I'm not sure why. It started a few years after Tony was first diagnosed. I heard the song on my car radio, and it literally took my breath away. I had to pull over to collect myself as I was hyperventilating and sobbing. Grief hits you hard sometimes when you least expect it. I had no idea why this song struck me so and still does. When I first heard it, I imagined myself years down the road, explaining to people just how I cured Tony's autism. I imagined how happy I would be, and Tony would be by my side, smiling, with his arm around me, proud as could be. He'd be *normal*. He'd be in high school.

But back to today. I heard the song on my way to pick up Tony from school—from high school. He is not cured. Nor may he ever be.

The song is simple, really. It's about time grabbing you by the wrist and happening right before your eyes, even when you're not paying attention. It's about life being unpredictable, yet realizing that the blessings are truly in the journey. It's about acceptance and trusting that God has a specific plan in place for you.

Now when I hear the lyrics, I dream of a day when Tony will be able to live symptom-free, knowing in my heart that he will never fully be free of autism.

A simple song, a simple dream, adapted with time.

aDS foR gRaDS

DECEMBER 7, 2010

If you're a parent of a senior in high school, you know that this year is full of deadlines. Ads for Grads is one of them in our community. Every year, the yearbook staff sponsors a fundraiser. You may choose to submit an AD as part of the celebration for your senior. These advertisements are a unique part of the yearbook in that they add a very personal, heartfelt touch to your senior's yearbook by looking back on their early years. You must include a photo of your son or daughter in his or her younger years. An AD for Grad is a wonderful way to say something important to your son or daughter— such as some sound advice or just how much you love them—before he or she graduates. All proceeds from these ads help supplement the costs of the yearbook.

This particular assignment was given to me the summer before Tony's senior year. It haunted me all summer. The deadline was upon me, and I had almost six months to prepare. Why was this deadline so hard for me this time? With my oldest, I just made a quick decision, wrote something witty (or so I thought), and off it went. But with Tony, it wasn't that easy. I'm sure I was overthinking it. I couldn't help it. And every time I went to choose a picture or choose a saying, I started crying. Every single time. I mean, this is a child that will actually *look* at his yearbook year after year. He studies faces, names, and compares them to other years to see just how everyone changed over the years. He will use this book for the rest of his life. This is a child who had so many people helping him along the way. This is a child who made his mark on the entire school district (and the crisis team, thank you). This is a child who didn't just slide through; this took a huge team of professionals with countless hours of planning and strategizing and tons and tons of patience. I knew I needed to say something that he could relate to, yet so could all the adults who've helped him along the way. I couldn't use clichés, or any play on words. I couldn't use some profound saying that didn't have any meaning to him. I wanted it to be something that represented *him*—something that, when he read it over and over again, he would smile and think, "Yes. That is me. I can do that."

So I started researching Disney quotes or anything from Walt Disney and Pixar and anything Hollywood

or movie related. I had so many choices. "Here's looking at you, kid," or "Follow the yellow brick road," or
"Did you rub my lamp? Did you wake me up? Did you
bring me here? And all of a sudden you're walking out
on me? I don't think so, not right now!" Okay, I got
carried away. That was from *Aladdin*. Or how about
"Anyone who gave you confidence, you owe them a lot"
(Breakfast at Tiffany's)?

Also running through my head were *my* favorite
quotes: "The only disability in life is a bad attitude,"
"Never doubt your abilities," "All your dreams can come
true if you have the courage to pursue them," "If you
can dream it, you can do it" (all from Walt Disney.)

Or these: "Anything is possible, if you just believe"
(*Polar Express*); "Do what you can, with what you have,
where you are" (Unknown); "I can do all things through
Christ who strengthens me" (Philippians 4:13); or my
very favorite, "What we can easily see is only a small
percentage of what is possible. Imagination is having the vision to see what is just below the surface: to
picture that which is essential but invisible to the eye"
(Unknown).

That's my Tony. There's so much more than what is
visible. It's like he's trapped, and not yet tapped. But all
of that was too deep for him, too abstract and not vis-
ual. So after months of debating, overthinking, search-
ing for pictures, and putting this off, I turned it in. I
chose a picture that was right in front of me, hanging
on my wall, and a quote from *Toy Story* that I heard
Tony saying on an old family video tape we watched
over the Thanksgiving holiday.

To my Tony,

To infinity and beyond! We'll be with you every
step of the way.

Love,
Mom, Dad, Michael,
Joey, and yes, even Beau

And I cried the whole time I wrote it.

Vaccinations

JANUARY 11, 2011

It has to be said; there is so much controversy out there right now arguing whether vaccines play a role in the outbreak of autism. People are spouting their opinions about an old study found to be fraudulent. Truth be told, it's just too much stress for me to even take this on. I lost too much sleep over it years ago, and now it just makes me angry. *Something* is causing autism. Vaccines are big business. How could we ever take them on? They help many, but are we so ignorant to think that they will not harm any? I know the numbers of those harmed are low in comparison, but what if *you* become a number? And why is that number growing at such a rapid pace?

I'm sickened by all the finger-pointing. I'm tired of studies done to prove that vaccines are not the cause of autism. All I know is, consequently, Tony's first few signs of autism happened shortly after he received a vaccination at eighteen months when he was on an antibiotic, sick with an ear infection. Coincidental? Not sure. Is it what caused his autism? Only one person can answer that for me, and someday when I stand before Him, my Lord and Savior, I'll get my answer. But will I point a finger and blame vaccinations? No. I won't. My stand is simply this: vaccinations may have played a part in Tony's autism. It may be a piece of the puzzle. Would I choose to vaccinate again? I already did. Both of Tony's brothers received all of their vaccinations. One is older, one is younger. However, with our younger son, I was extremely knowledgeable and insistent that they separate all vaccines and do them on our own time schedule, making sure he was strong and healthy when he received them. Neither of Tony's brothers have autism.

I know I open myself up to criticism, but frankly, I'm just too exhausted to argue anymore. I'm more focused on how we survive. Was it *the* cause? We may never know. But in the meantime, can we all quit fighting over this subject and just get to work on finding a solution? A cure? Please? And I'll do my best to help him survive through diet, nutritional supplements, therapies, and everything else under the sun available to me that great people have created to help us parents cope with autism. Just my thoughts.

The WONDeR of PaRaPRofessiONaLS aND TeacheRs

JANUARY 19, 2011

As I was digging through a closet last weekend, I happened upon a large stack of notebooks that literally took my breath away. They were all from Tony's elementary school years. One of the best communication tools we used back then was a notebook that would travel with Tony to and from school. His paraprofessionals (or paras, as we lovingly call them) would write me detailed notes of Tony's school day since Tony could not communicate that with us. Back and forth it would go, filled with the good, the not-so-good, and even the very bad things that happened each day. To say that it was important to us is an understatement. It was the only way we could have an insight as to what was happening at school and how Tony was progressing. It took patience and dedication from these awesome paras to take the time during what I'm sure was a very hectic day to write a note to us. I looked forward to it every day, and I always wrote back. The nice thing about those notebooks is that I have a slice of time that I can look back on and remember.

I always say that I have a gift of being able to forget the stressful times and move on. I'm sure I haven't forgotten them; I'm just able to put them aside and move on to the next adventure. It's the only way I can do it. Sometimes I don't want to recall, but other times I do. It's nice to see all the progress we've made over the years, still knowing there's so far yet to go. Here's the very first page of his second grade notebook. (Keep in mind, back twelve or thirteen years ago, autism was not in the spotlight or as common as it sadly is now.)

Tips for Tony

1. When watching a video, Tony likes to watch and listen to the *very* end. He will get very upset if the video is stopped and done so without warning.

2. Tony loves the computer. It is a good calming tool.

3. A good technique for Tony is "First _____, then _____." (i.e., "first math time, then recess!")

4. Tony may need a few verbal cues before cooperating. He cannot "read" social cues but will mimic someone who is upset or happy.

5. Tony needs and seeks out big, strong hugs for approval and acceptance. It's also good for calming.

6. If overstimulated or overwhelmed, Tony may lose his cool. Be firm and stay calm. He is learning to calm himself. He will feel bad about it after and may need some physical time (i.e., swinging, jumping, running).

7. Last year, they used PECS (picture exchange communication system) to help him learn his schedule. If something will be changing, just give him verbal warnings.

"Today is going to be different, Tony."

Here's another entry from September 22, 2000:

I want to tell you how wonderful Tony is! Every day, we are seeing progress. He is adapting to schedule changes throughout the day, answering questions with yes or no, sitting quietly in a large group, making eye contact when Mrs. J is speaking, and the list goes on and on. He makes us smile all the time!

I want to commend Mrs. E for caring for Tony so much! She is doing a wonderful job mainstreaming Tony into the regular education classroom. She works very hard to make each day go smoothly! Gracias, Mrs. E! You are appreciated! (This is the year Tony learned to speak Spanish. Mrs. E was bilingual.)

—Mrs. S

I believe I cried when I read that. We were struggling so hard in those early years just to get Tony to cooperate and just *be* in our world. So I'd like to find all of Tony's paras and teachers from all his years in school— including the early intervention at age two, from 1995 to 2011—and express my gratitude to each and every one of them. We could not have made this journey without them! We know just what a little stinker our Toneman can be, and we know that their job was not easy. Rewarding? Yes. Easy? Not for a minute.

As we near the last few months of Tony's high school days, I can't help but wonder how lucky we were through the years to have such great paras.

If you are reading this and you're one of them, God bless you. We thank you for your dedication to our Toneman.

aTTiTUDe

JANUARY 26, 2011

It's been another tumultuous few weeks here for no particular reason, except maybe a full moon? He's been breaking things, crashing lightbulbs on the floor, trying to start bonfires or light candles, feeding the dog all of his gluten-free food. I seriously could go on and on. I have this nagging headache that won't go away, and I know what it is. Worry. Frustration. Fear. Sometimes, this autism thing can really burn you out. But as I sit at my computer tonight, I couldn't help thinking of my favorite quotes is by Scott Hamilton: "The only disability in life is a bad attitude." I recite this to myself many times during the day. It's very true. Attitude can make or break your day, your life, your future. One of the things posted in my office is the following poem that keeps me grounded:

> The longer I live, the more I realize the impact
> of Attitude on life. Attitude, to me, is more

important than facts. It is more important than the past, than education, than money, than circumstances, than failures, than successes, than what other people think or say or do. It is more important than appearance, giftedness, or skill. It will make or break a company...a church...a home. The remarkable thing is we have a choice every day regarding the attitude we will embrace for that day. We cannot change our past...we cannot change the fact that people will act in a certain way. We cannot change the inevitable. The only thing we can do is play on the one string we have, and that is our Attitude. I am convinced that life is 10 percent what happens to me and 90 percent how I react to it. And so it is with you...we are in charge of our Attitudes.

—Charles R. Swindoll

I hope this helps you as much as it has helped me today, and many days in the past.

Oh, Lord, grant me patience for all my blessings.

To the Mom in the Waiting Room

FEBRUARY 2, 2011

I want to apologize to the mom in the waiting room at the doctor's clinic. We went for a visit this morning to have Tony's ears checked again. We just finished a round of antibiotics for a severe ear infection in his left ear. Yes, he is still plagued with ear infections at age seventeen; not as often, but when they come, it's always severe. Now, it's hit his right ear. A trip to the doctor is no picnic. Not only does Tony sometimes forget his inner voice, but he also has *zero* tolerance for crying babies, or whining toddlers, or screaming four-year-olds. But we love his pediatrician, and then we realize that when he turns eighteen next month, he'll need to find an adult doctor. But I just can't make a change right now. Not yet. There are just too many changes going on this year for him. We'll tackle that one later.

So we walked into the building—and mind you, it was incredibly cold outside—and Tony was dragging his feet, taking his time, moping. Just like a typical teenager. No time schedule. No sense of urgency. No enthusiasm. He only kept telling me that his right ear is "burning," which is a new word choice for him—I'm happy with that, but I was running late. Down the hall he went, then he decided to speak in an unrecognizable foreign language and in a very loud animated fashion with hand gestures and songs to everyone who passes by. It just so happened to be a very busy day at the doctor's office. Heads turned—some stared, some giggled, and some frowned.

"Come on, Tone. Let's hurry!" I said as I ground my teeth with a smile. I knew he was testing my patience—again. Then I heard it. I heard a toddler in the waiting area. He's screaming at the top of his lungs. My Tony, all six feet and two hundred pounds of him, ran down the hall to the toddler with his hands over his ears, yelling, "*Stop screaming! Knock it off, please!*" And then he added some of that unrecognizable language. I thought the little boy was going to cry, but he looked way up at Tony, and all he said was, "'kay." I was devastated—but I'm used to it—and wanted to apologize to his mom, but by the time I redirected Tony and calmed him down, she was gone.

What is it about that pitch that bothers him so much? I'm sure it's like any unexpected noise or anything that startles him, but he's so darn sensitive to that. And how is that avoidable? It used to be an issue, then I thought he grew out of it, but now it's back.

That's another thing about autism. You can teach him a skill like riding a bike or tying his shoes right on schedule, but down the road he may lose it. Why is it then that other things like dates and historical facts are permanently filed in his brain? I guess that's just another piece of the puzzle.

As the nurse called our name, she smiled and said, "What language are we using today, Tony?"

"Hebrew," he said.

Go figure.

a WORK iN PROGRESS

FEBRUARY 4, 2011

Our wedding anniversary is always a special day in our house. We usually watch our wedding video, look at photo albums with Tony, and reminisce about that special day. For just a minute, I want to let you know about my husband, who is the silent partner of this journey. Back in 1995 when Tony was first diagnosed, one of the professionals working on Tony's program told us that most marriages with a special needs child will end in divorce. It's usually too stressful, financially devastating, and most of the time, the couple will disagree on discipline strategies or therapies. (Wow, thanks for the head's-up. Any other good news?) I remember having this conversation with Dave shortly after hearing that Tony was diagnosed with PDD-NOS (pervasive developmental delay-not otherwise specified), which, by the way, I could not accept as autism as I was still in denial. Dave was the one with the level head and the one to go to the library and research the subject. I, however, cried for weeks. In fact, if my memory serves me right, I even threw the book at him that he brought home for me to read, screaming, "Our son is not autistic! He is not Rainman!"

My husband is the one who listens to my ideas, plans, therapies, research, and frustrations day in and day out. He is the one who encourages me to write. He is the one who has seen me at my lowest points, yet still manages to get me to laugh. Although these years will go down silently in our own family's history books, what I want the world to know is that I could not have gotten through it without him. We make a fantastic team. Maybe that's why we were destined to meet all those years ago in the bar of a restaurant. It still amazes me how God could send me someone so perfect for this job. Has it been easy? Of course not. No marriage is. Do we agree on everything we do for Tony? Not for a minute. Do we try to hear each other's opinions? Most of the time. Do we have a long road ahead of us? Absolutely. I think what has gotten us through these years is that we surround ourselves with loving family members and trusted friends. We have the best support system a couple could ever ask for. And for that, we are eternally thankful. We had no idea what was in store for us all those year ago. No one ever does. But none-theless, I'm still praying for more of the same.

Happy anniversary, honey, and make sure you buckle up. This ride's not over.

check YOUR ego aT The DOOR

FEBRUARY 12, 2011

One of the things most parents raising kids with autism know well is the constant embarrassment or humiliation that goes with the territory. The calls from school, the looks, the stares, the general inappropriateness of everything that child does, especially in public. Yes, we've tried teaching them everything you did with your child as they were growing up. The problem is, with autism, kids lose their skills. They are socially inept. And it doesn't bother them. But it might bother the parents and the siblings.

It's hard for the parent or caregiver to take them public places and deal with the inappropriateness and the social disgrace. In the beginning, I was devastated. I'm a very social person, always have been. I thrive on being the entertainer and being entertained. I'm what they call an influencer, energetic, imaginative, someone who focuses on the new and the future, focused on people rather than tasks, according to the widely used personality type tests. So what does it mean to "check your ego at the door"? It means to get out of your own stinkin' way. It's not about you. So stop thinking it is.

My husband and I went to a seminar back in 2003 that taught us both this concept. The seminar had nothing to do with autism but everything to do with how to live through it. We went to this seminar with friends thinking we were going for business. We ended up being there for survival. What we learned in that short weekend was nothing short of a miracle. We learned that the gifts we were given were for a larger purpose. Our natural positive attitudes and zest for life were there for a reason, so we could endure when times were so tough that we didn't want to face another day. The gift I think we have is that we can find humor in every situation, and that we are strong in social situations, therefore, we can overcome the awkwardness and get on to the business of teaching our children the very things they need to survive in our socially driven world. Am I saying that only certain people can survive raising a child with autism? No. What I'm saying is that this is just how we've managed to survive.

So last week, as I rushed to school to help in a crisis situation with Tony, I literally checked my ego at the door. I steadied my emotions, thanked the crisis team on the way in, who were also there to help, and proceeded to calm Tony enough to take him home. It's so not about me. Every parent will tell you that. The difference here is that I've had to get over caring about what everyone else thinks. And that's not easy. I've had to get over the humiliation and the frustration because this is not the first time something devastating has happened. And it most likely won't be the last.

TONYiSMS

FEBRUARY 17, 2011

Our Tony is famous in our family for creating his own expressions. Since his language literally disappeared between the age of one and two, he has never really caught up despite the triumphant efforts of many speech therapists, teachers, and family. How he has coped is by creating his own one or two-liners—what we lovingly call "Tonyisms." I'll share some of these along the way, but yesterday's made me smile and I thought you'd enjoy it. Tony was getting ready in our bathroom yesterday, as usual, and I heard some rattling. He came down to the kitchen carrying three lightbulbs from the vanity. He handed them to me and proudly said, "The battery's out!"

You gotta love this guy.

MORE TONYISMS

FEBRUARY 22, 2011

A typical conversation between me and my almost-eighteen-year-old at bedtime goes something like this:

> "I'm sick for the school tomorrow," Tony announces as I tuck his weighted blanket in on top of him.
>
> "What about Rachel? She will miss you," I say, smiling.
>
> "He's sick." (Pronouns are still hard for him.)
>
> "*She's* not sick, silly. What about Michelle? She'll miss you too."
>
> "He's sick."
>
> "*She's* not sick," I say yet again as I correct him.
>
> "*Yes!* He's sick! Are you nuts?" (A lovely phrase he now uses at all times when he doesn't like what I have to say. At this point, he's testing my patience.)
>
> "Well, what about Rob and Nick?" I ask.

"Sick. And sick."

"Hmmm… Well then… We can't go to see Marni tomorrow. That's a bummer." Marni cuts his hair. She's very pretty, and he loves her.

(Long pause.)

"How 'bout school?" I smile and leave the room.

Ten minutes later.

"Mommy! Mommy! Can you hear me?" he yells as he knocks on the wall. Keep in mind, he only calls me Mommy when he wants something.

"Yes, Tony. What do you need?" I say loudly through the wall.

"Good night, Mommy. [Pause.] Mommy? *Mommy*? Come in here now, *please*!" I get out of bed and walk in his room.

"Yes?" I sigh.

"Go see Marni?" he whispers.

"Yes, Tony. We'll see Marni tomorrow. Go to sleep now," I say, shutting the door.

Five minutes later.

"Mommy? *Mommy*?" He says loudly as he knocks on the wall again.

"*Good night, Tony!*" I say with my best patient hat on.

"Good night, Mommy!" This continues for a bit, and he finally falls asleep.

I'm seriously considering some sleep medication for *myself*.

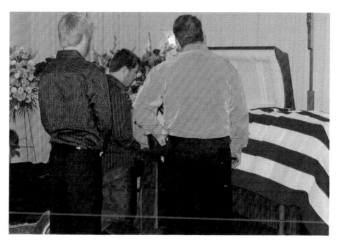

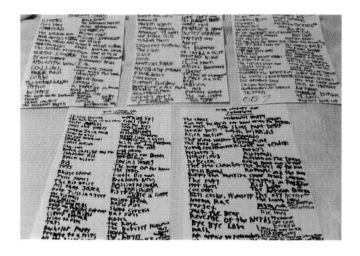

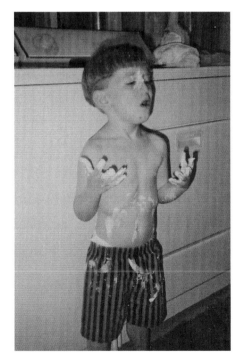

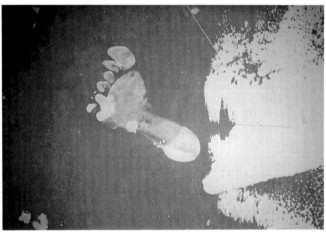

GRANDMA PAT

MARCH 15, 2011

We lost Tony's Grandma Pat shortly after Grandpa Gene died to what we believe was literally a broken heart. As you recall, Grandpa Gene died a few months prior, and we were so proud of how Tony handled the funeral and his death. Just five short months later, Grandpa Gene's wife of fifty years joined him in heaven. Grandma Pat had a stroke, which lead to a heart attack, while attending mass on a Sunday morning.

Looking back, we now see the signs that her heart was failing in more ways than one. It's a beautiful story, actually. Grandma Pat told us that she talked to Grandpa Gene. That she dreamt of him, talked to him, and then finally, she saw him in the living room. That he had come for her. I truly think that her heart was so lonely for him and the life they had that she was ready to go with him. Grandma Pat claimed her Irish heritage with pride. I'll never forget the day our Tony was born. She couldn't have been prouder. Anthony Patrick "Tony" Becker was born on St. Patrick's Day 1993, and I believe my mother-in-law was in our room about two minutes after he was born bearing all things Irish.

Having just been through the funeral experience, Tony was once again a trooper. We had a private viewing for him, and he was so very sad. He understood he was saying good-bye forever. We celebrated her life with a theme of green and even made sure she was wearing her shamrock socks. Later that week, I found Tony reading this in one of his *Book of Saints*:

Why a shamrock?

St. Patrick used the shamrock to explain the Trinity, and has been associated with him and the Irish since that time.

St. Patrick was a humble, pious, gentle man, whose love and total devotion to and trust in God should be a shining example to each of us. He feared nothing, not even death, so complete was his trust in God, and of the importance of his mission.

We'll miss you, Grandma Pat. We promise to carry on your wishes and to *always* celebrate all things Irish!

TONY TURNS eighTeeN

MARCH 20, 2011

It's always hard for a parent to celebrate milestone birthdays with their kids, like turning eighteen years old, because deep down, we still see them as our adorable little munchkin. It would be so wonderful to be able to scoop Tony up in my arms, squeeze his cheek next to mine in front of the mirror, and say, "Who's so handsome?" "Me am!" he would say, smiling proudly. Except there will be no scooping up a two-hundred-pound, six-foot eighteen-year-old this year. Instead, I had asked Tony months ago to think about what his eighteenth-year birthday wish would be. And I would try hard to make that wish come true.

Tony turned eighteen years old on St. Patrick's Day. We had been talking about it for some time, and his anxiety was climbing. He was so excited to wake up that day. He rushed into my bathroom and looked straight into the mirror, saying, "Bigger?" He showered, shaved, left a huge mess, and got all dressed up in green. I love it when he understands milestones. His wish this year was as simple as ever. He only wanted one thing. He wanted to go stay at a hotel. And he wanted to bring our dog, Beau. Simple, right? Well, kind of. It took a few phone calls to find a hotel that not only accepts pets, but one that would accept our hundred-pound Lab. We found one not too far from our house. I booked two adjoining rooms so Tony feel grown-up and independent. I also wanted to make sure he had his own space to set up his DVDs and books and a place to have his snacks so he won't be disrupted by any outside noises. It was just how he liked it. A perfect night. Beau settled in pretty quickly also, and got a little too comfortable.

All in all, it was a great night. Just Tony, his dog, his family in the next room, and his new DVD collection. And as requested, we picked up some chips and salsa, chicken fajitas, popcorn, and a gluten-free chocolate cake. So while Tony and Beau settled into their own room to watch his new World War I, World War II, and classic Hollywood DVDs, the rest of us stayed in the adjoining room watching our own movie marathon. What a great way to spend a Saturday night together. Well, kind of together.

TOP TEN THINGS TO DO WHILE EVERYONE ELSE IS ON SPRING BREAK

MARCH 27, 2011

Seriously, my neighborhood is deserted. This is just not right. This is my take on keeping my sense of humor while everyone else is enjoying the sun, and I'm stuck here in the winter tundra with dreams of someday finding an overnight personal care attendant that I trust so we could leave on vacation. But until then, here are my suggestions for having fun while everyone else has fled the cold:

10. Get a manicure and pedicure; ask for the *tropical package.*

9. Catch up on your Facebook creeping. *Wear your sunglasses as a disguise.*

8. Pick up the dog poo in the yard that has now surfaced from melting snow. *Wear shorts and sandals.*

7. Deep clean the oven in your bathing suit. *Feel the heat.*

6. Go to happy hour and order a Sea Breeze or Bahama Mama. *Bring your beach hat.*

5. Drive with your convertible top down sporting mittens and a parka. *Wear sunscreen strictly for the coconut smell.*

4. Color your gray-haired roots. *Put a little lemon juice in there too, in case a sunbeam comes through the window.*

3. Sweep the sand in the garage into a pile, put up lawn chairs, and light your tiki lights from last summer. *Play a little of Jimmy Buffett's "Margaritaville" loudly.*

2. Take a mental vacation. Watch *Couple's Retreat.* It takes place in Bora Bora. *Sip a fruity cocktail.*

And the number 1 thing to do on spring break while everyone else is getting much-needed vitamin D:

1. Research destinations for next year's spring break trip. Book the sitter.

That's all I'm sayin'. There is simply nothing like beach therapy. I need to go to my happy place.

a DiffeReNT abiLiTY

APRIL 10, 2011

I sit in my newly cleaned office, listening to Tony through the ceiling. He's reciting a movie, word for word, and having a ball upstairs. The feelings I have are so extreme. One minute I'm laughing with him, and the next my thoughts are wandering off on how others his age are getting ready for prom and senior skip day, getting jobs, and choosing colleges. It's bittersweet because I am totally entertained by his Hollywood performance, yet mourning the loss of what could have been. I know that this autism does not define him. I know that. I do. But it does define how we live our lives. I'm not saying that in a negative way. I'm just pointing out the fact that we've all adapted. This means the ordinary sights, sounds, smells, tastes, and touches of everyday life that you may not even notice can be downright painful for him. We know that, and we automatically adjust as quickly as we can.

I used to laugh and say that I was Tony's interpreter. One of my college majors was a foreign language. Interestingly enough, I lived in a foreign country and studied abroad during college. Most of the people I came in contact with did not speak English, so I got really good at reading body language and interpreting language. And I got good at speaking *their* language. Oh, how that skill has helped me in raising Tony. My life was perfectly carved for this role, and I'm right where I'm supposed to be. The day I realized that, I believe, was the first day I really accepted autism into the family. I've learned to slow down and to speak directly in plain, simple words. Don't get me wrong, I can still be a chatty person. Ask any of my friends. But I've adapted with Tony because that's the only way I can communicate with him. And I want that more than anything.

Tony interprets language literally. So I think about every word I say to him before I say it. I want him to understand and be able to speak back to me. Sometimes, this is simply exhausting. But it's always worthwhile. We've learned to be patient with his limited vocabulary. It's hard for him to describe his feelings. He may be hungry, frustrated, scared, or uninterested, have a head-ache or a stomachache, but those words are beyond his ability to express. I watch for agitation or frustra-tion when he can't express himself. I can usually sense his anxiety climbing, and we try very hard to catch it before it becomes a disaster. If you can figure out how meltdowns occur, they can be prevented. That is magical when it happens. And that is a million-dollar skill to possess. Patience is truly a virtue and a learned skill, and in this case, a necessity. Work to view autism as a different, special ability rather than a disability. Because as an interpreter, there are many things they can teach *you*.

The WhY

APRIL 15, 2011

I read another autism article recently that talked about having PTSD (post-traumatic stress disorder) and reliving the reality of this disorder day in and day out. And they weren't talking about the kids. They were talking about the parents who are raising the kids with autism. I haven't been able to get that article out of my mind. I do believe that there are many moments that I relive, or recreate, the sadness and trauma of the moment we were given this diagnosis. At the time, I thought it was literally unthinkable and that I could *fix* him. And the deep, deep desire we have to help him reach his potential, whatever that may be. I was familiar with the sleepless nights, the anxiety, the sensory overload, the fear, the panic, and the mental exhaustion that they were talking about in the article.

What's it like living with PTSD? Well, I frankly don't know any other life, so at times it's exhilarating and at other times not so much. That doesn't sound so far from *normal*, does it? All I want is for my child to be happy and successful. That's no different than any other parent. My blessing just might take a little more effort, and I guess someone thought I was qualified for the job. That's my *why*. That's what gets me up every morning and gets me through every challenge. Of course, I can't help but wonder what my Tony would be like if he *were* normal and could really communicate. What would he say? What would he tell me? I would walk a thousand miles just to be able to have a conversation with him about what he's feeling and why he gets so frustrated at times. Maybe he could help answer the one question that's been burning on my mind since his diagnosis some seventeen years ago. Why did this happen? Or maybe he'll tell me that the *why* just doesn't really matter.

UNWRiTTeN

APRIL 27, 2011

It's been a difficult couple of weeks. Tony is officially done with high school, and we are taking a couple of days (weeks, months) to process that. On Monday, he starts his "college orientation" (that's what we're calling it because, logically, that's what his big brother did) for his transitional program, which he will be in until he's twenty-one years old. We are excited, but anticipating change always makes a tense environment here. Although he's ready for a new routine, sadness overwhelms me at times that high school is over for him, and it just wasn't *normal*. I realize these are my issues, not his, as we stretch into the new routine, paving our way into the unknown. Who knows where this will take him. And like most high school seniors, his life is still unwritten.

I find many signs that the good Lord is speaking to me, telling me that it's all going to be okay. I can sense that there's so many words up in his head and so many conversations going on sometimes, yet he can't converse. I can't imagine how frustrating that is. Is he waiting for this to go away and be fixed? Or has he already embraced it?

This is what I would tell him, and it took me a very long time to get here. "It is what it is. It's just the beginning. Go create your story. No one else can do it for you. Release your inhibitions, stop letting other things hold you back. Stop worrying about what everyone else is thinking, just lay it out there, and embrace it. This is *your* gift. Go make it worthy."

And that goes for anyone—in your job, the business you just started, your kids, your spouse or even your "self,"—and especially your life with autism. Just my thoughts as the story unfolds…

iT HaPPeNeD oNe DaY

JUNE 1, 2011

Sometimes, life throws you a curve ball, and it's up to you to decide if you're going to duck or if you stand strong and face it head-on. Sometimes, that's a split-second decision, and other times, it's a lifelong decision. These are words from my introduction, words that have again showed themselves to be true last month. I've been waiting to have the nerve to share with you all what happened at Tony's new school last month. I almost thought it was too private, but then the more I thought about it, the more felt I should share it, especially for those of you reading this who are raising children with autism. This happens. It's not pretty. It's heartbreaking, but it happens. I'm not afraid to share it anymore. I feel like those of us with older kids on the spectrum are somewhat of a pioneer and have literally fought for things that are now not only covered by insurance, but are much more accepted than they were seventeen years ago. I'm certainly not saying that what I'm sharing with you below is socially acceptable. I'm just saying that when this happens, or if this ever happens to you, please know that you're not alone. That someone else out there who's devoted their lives to beating this autism-thing is breaking down barriers, and praying for strength, just like you.

Here's our story. It's not pretty, but it's real.

Let me set the scene. Tony had started at a new transitional program about fours days before this incident. It was going phenomenally well. We hadn't seen him that happy in years, he was genuinely smiling so hard that we could see his dimples! I'd forgotten just how cute that smile was. We have no idea what caused this meltdown. No triggers other than he just didn't want to go home that day. One theory is the online rumors that were surfacing about the "end of the world" or that "judgment day" was approaching, and he wanted to research it but ran out of time that day. Remember, he's very literal.

This is why autism is so hard. He doesn't lie, and he doesn't understand lies. Everything is black and white. The mystery is to figure out the missing pieces of this thought pattern because he's unable to communicate that with us.

Below is an e-mail that I wrote to two of my best friends the next day.

To my girls:

Thank you so much for your messages and texts… I reached out to you two in a desperate moment as I was headed to the new program for Tony which teaches him steps toward adult responsibilities until he's 21 yrs old. He was not ready to go home yesterday, and for some reason, it turned into a bloody, horrific meltdown. The mother of all meltdowns. Because they are off school property (but still a part of the district), they had to call for backup when he got physically violent and started to really hurt himself... banging his head so hard they thought the windows were going to shatter, throwing things, etc... They called 911 and me. By the time I got there, there were 5 police cars and an ambulance.

You can imagine my heart-wrenching reaction and even disbelief. I ran upstairs and what I saw was just more than I can even describe. My child... my baby... my man-boy... being restraint by police officers, blood all over his body from a cut, his forehead slightly swollen, screams and rage, and a torn up sensory room. All the district teachers and paras were a wreck—even the men. Everyone was shocked that our happy guy turned inside out so quickly. When Tony saw me, he started crying out "Help me! Help me, Mommy!" I don't think I'll ever get that image out of my mind.

When things calmed down for a second, the police officers said they wanted to take him via ambulance to the ER because they thought he needed stitches in his finger, which we think he cut on the window shades during his rage. The only way to do that was to sedate him. They wouldn't release him to me for my safety. So I watched, in horror, as they held down my child and gave him a shot of a tranquilizer and an amnesia drug so he would not remember the trauma. With a fight, he was out in just a matter of minutes. It was so frightening to watch.

I texted you both on my way to the ER—at the stoplight—with my police escort, which in hindsight, was probably not the right thing to do—the texting while getting a police escort thing. Whoops.

I prayed all the way just asking for guidance, strength, and the ability to get through this without breaking down. I did it. But am feeling the after effects today and I'm a blubbering mess.

They had to give Tony another round of tranquilizers and the other drug a few hours later so we could get through the psych eval and the paperwork. He did not need stitches (thank God, because he would have picked them off anyway). We talked with an emergency psychiatrist who, for some reason, thought I was new to this autism thing and asked if I'd ever heard of sensory integration. I didn't want to snap back with an answer that I think I could write a book about that subject, given our sixteen year history with sensory integration, so I just smiled and said we'd definitely look into it. She then gave me the phone number to The Autism Society (which was already on speed dial on my cell phone…) and released us.

Whatever… the best thing she did was give us a small prescription for a mild sedative to help with sleep and anxiety when we see him progressing toward a meltdown. That should get us to next Wednesday, when we have an emergency appointment with a psychiatrist to give us a better prescription—something to help his angry and violent outbursts and self injurious tendencies—and for our own safety. I don't know what else we can do.

In the meantime, the Autism Society called me back this morning and they are going to help me get Tony on a waitlist for a specialty psychiatrist that deals with these very things and works with adults with autism. They are also helping us find permanent placement for him someday. This may be sooner than I had hoped...

I can't imagine that day...

Can a person's heart break in more than one place? Because I think mine has.

I didn't intend to get this detailed with you, but now that I have, I strangely feel a little better. Plus, I will be able to have a record of this in my files for "someday."

I'm scared of the consequences of yesterday's actions. I'm scared for Tony and for us. I hope we find some medication that will allow his brain to turn off all the "voices" and for him to be able to function from day to day. He's so intelligent and such a wonderful person. We don't get to see that much and it breaks my heart. He was having such great days at his new college—heavenly days to the point that I was finally so happy that he found a home. Like I said, we saw his adorable dimples and he was genuinely smiling and happy. Fortunately, he is not kicked out of the program. They are so forgiving and it's not the first time this happened and it probably won't be the last.

All I know is, there are truly angels working here on earth. I could not do their job. I'm so thankful that there are people like that willing to help kids like mine…

As always, I trust your confidence. I haven't even told my parents yet because I don't want to frighten them and frankly, I tend to sob like a little child when I try to tell my Mom because I let my guard down. I will tell them—just not right this second…

Thanks for being there for me and thanks for caring so much. Xoxo. Love you both. p.s. the graduation party is on hold…

(Wipe tears.)

Update:

I am happy to report that in the weeks that have passed, Tony is like a new kid. He's happy, tolerant, conversational, funny, witty, and patient. He's not perfect, by any means. But he's teachable. And that's all we're asking for. I think we have our son back, and that's all that really matters, right?

Thanks for listening, and most importantly, keep the faith. I know I will.

a STanDiNg OvaTioN

JULY 1, 2011

A few years ago at my company's convention, they brought a family on stage in front of over eight thousand people and awarded them the Spirit Award. This award goes to leaders who have overcome heavy obstacles and adversities in their lives and lead with integrity and spirit to help others. This family had a teenage son with autism. When they brought the son on stage, a loud cheer erupted, and the crowd rose to their feet and gave him a standing ovation. I wept in my seat. In fact, I wept so hard that I had to remove myself and find a dark, quiet place in the back of the room to release my emotions. Because it was at that moment that I realized my Tony was more severe than I'd ever let on.

Grief hits you at strange times, and when it does, you just have to let it come.

What I realized is that I had to toughen up, admit it, and find him the help he deserves. I wanted Tony to someday have that standing ovation. I wanted him to be able to someday get on a stage and tell his story. But my Tony could never do that, at least not now. He could not handle the crowd, the noise, the lights, or the over-stimulation that comes with a crowded room. I realized that day that Tony was not as high-functioning as he used to be. I realized that I was never going to be able to *fix* him. I had reached acceptance. It had been a very long road. And I knew we still had a lot of work to do.

Now, I'd like to give Tony that standing ovation. We had a small graduation party for him on June 4, just for immediate family and a few neighbors that surround our house. Neighbors who have welcomed Tony into their house, whether he was invited or not, and neighbors who have watched Tony grow up and have been another set of eyes for us through the years.

The day went so smoothly, and I was so very proud of my Toneman. He greeted everyone who came, sat out front watching cars go by hoping they were coming to his party, and he opened every single card right there on the spot. I know this was hard for him, and I know there was a lot of anticipation surrounding this day, but he really pulled it off. It was a great day, and we were all so proud!

So without further ado, I'd like to welcome to the "stage," Mr. Tony Becker!

Well done, Toneman! Well done!

The Thank-you Note

JULY 7, 2011

As we wrap up the graduation season, I wanted to share this. Tony was so proud of the thank-you note that he wrote below. I verbally asked him to just say "Thank you for the graduation gift," and we'd make copies for everyone. But he added the last part and drew the pictures of what I'm guessing is his *college*.

Just to note, getting Tony to write anything is no small feat. I think he enjoyed the process of "the thank-you note" as he so lovingly called it. He would sit for long periods of time, folding each note, stuffing the envelope, placing the address label on, some straighter than others, placing *his* return label on and then adding the stamp. He had our entire dining room table all set up with his process. And he worked diligently on it for a week straight.

Getting the mail is still a highlight of his day, but now that the graduation season is over, he's back to being excited about his daily newspaper, the *Tribune* and the *Herald* on Thursdays, and his *People* magazine on Fridays. Soon to start arriving is the *Smithsonian* magazine and more *National Geographics*, which he will love.

Thank you again to family, friends, and followers who continue to support us through this process of raising this incredible young man. Your comments, messages, and prayers mean more to us than you'll ever know.

Tony's *college* will be our school district's transitional program that will be available to him until he's twenty-one years old. I do still worry about the chance that it may not work out. As you all well know, he's had some tough behavioral times in the past few years at school, but I do feel more confident now that his new medications are a small miracle in our lives. And as I'm getting to know his new social worker and some other new people who have just came into our lives since Tony is officially an adult, I feel like we have a new team of angels on our side.

Thank you for
my gratuation gift.
Love,
Tony Becker

I'm off to collage
Fall 2011.

iT'S oKaY To
TaKe a BReaK

AUGUST 11, 2011

Today, I will not run from myself, my circumstances, or my feelings. I will be open to myself,
others, God, and life. I will trust that by facing
today to the best of my ability, I will acquire the
skills I need to face tomorrow.

—Author unknown

I've been absent for a bit mentally. I won't deny it. I
got a disturbing call at the end of July that puts all of
our plans for the next three years on hold. It was very
upsetting, and it took me down.

Shortly after, I left for our company's convention
and literally checked out. For four blissful days, there
was no talk about autism, nothing about IEPs, BIPs,
SSIs, ABAs, no PCAs or PRNs, nothing about melt-

downs or the 5-point scale. No talk about programming and staffing. No talk about transitions.

I left that behind to celebrate with my team and spend a wonderful long weekend with my hubby and close friends to build *us* up. I've learned that building yourself up is incredibly important to be able to continue on this journey. Take the time to take a break, whether it's alone or with your spouse. You have no idea now how important this will be later. Trust me. Take time to take a break.

So on our break, we set goals, made a plan, and even had time to dream. I learned that for every set back, there is a set up waiting to happen. What an inspiring thought! So I'm choosing to focus on the set up that is coming…for this too shall pass.

ONCE AGAIN, JUST LET IT BE

NOVEMBER 2, 2011

A good friend of mine reminded me that the purpose of this devotional is to share the good, the bad, and also the meaningful. It's been a trying two months. We are taking it day by day. I'd like to share some revelations and what brought me back to life today.

I spent the day with Tony on one of our field trips to the southern part of the state to visit one of his favorite aunts and, of course, his grandparents.

What I learned today from Tony are the following:

1. Life is about joy. Search for it. Do something different if you can't find it.

2. Family is important. Visit frequently, and study picture albums to catch up.

3. Take time and count the pumpkins.

4. When all else fails, play a Beatles song and dance in the car like no one's watching.

While riding again, I was reminded of whom to turn to in times of trouble, times of confusion, and times of not knowing what is next. I have no idea what lies ahead for Tony, but I do know that I have a team of faith-based people who will be there to lean on. And what we are doing now, unfortunately, cannot continue. There was no way to know unless we tried; there has to be something out there that won't be a struggle for Tony and for those of us who care for him.

Someone once told me that if a goal doesn't scare you, it's not big enough. I guess I'm on the right track then.

YOU aRe STRONG

NOVEMBER 4, 2011

I received an e-mail with the words below from a very dear friend of mine, and it really helped me. I think because Tony's behavior has been so difficult lately that I tend to put on a front, and I guess after a while it's pretty transparent. I tend to get wrapped up in my own stress, and I forget that everyone has their own crosses to bear. Yes, it's been difficult, and yes, we've been holding our breath just to get through each day. I sometimes wish that I could have a magic ball and get a glance at what's coming today. At least I could feel a little more prepared and put on my big girl pants and toughen up a little.

I love him so much, but things are getting tough to handle. He's fighting demons, and it's hard to watch. It's hard to keep others out of harm's way because when he has his meltdowns, it's not my Tony. So when I read this early this morning, it touched me deeply. And it made me realize that whatever crosses we may bear, we are not alone. So many others are going through their own pain *every single day.*

YOU ARE STRONG

✦✦✦✦✦✦✦✦✦✦✦✦✦✦✦✦✦✦✦✦✦✦

How often has it happened – an acquaintance hears
your story or sees your child and says, "I'm not as
strong as you. I could never deal with all the things
you deal with." And you shake your head modestly,
and brush it off, and maybe even feel a little
condescended to. ✦ ✦ ✦ But you know what? They're
right. You're strong. You're facing things that the
average parent doesn't even want to imagine, and
you're handling them. ✦ ✦ ✦ Whether you were strong
to begin with or had strength thrust upon you by
necessity, you're one strong parent, one strong person.
Your family needs that strength, your children thrive
on it. You may wish you never had to be so strong. But
appreciate that strength now. It makes you special.
Capable. A force to be reckoned with. ✦ ✦ ✦

—Author Unknown

So I'm paying it forward.

This is dedicated to the following:

My friend who cares for her sick parents, every single day.

My friend who lives with the fear of cancer, every single day.

My friend who is trying to be brave while she waits for her husband to return from Kuwait, every single day.

My friend who is raising her family alone while her husband is protecting our freedom, every single day.

My friend who invested heavily in a new business and is struggling in this economy.

My friend who couldn't have her own child, so she handpicked a gem and puts her needs first, every single day.

My friend who gave up her career to care for a disabled child and tells him she loves him, every single day.

My friend who has an incredible job but mourns the time she loses with her children, every single day.

And to my friends who are raising kids like mine who get up and start over, every single day.

We all suffer in some way. What keeps me going is surrounding myself with incredibly strong people who will not only laugh with me, but will share their personal stress as if to say "I feel your pain."

My husband told me this morning that God only gives these challenges to people that He knows can handle them. So consider yourself blessed. And remember, you can make or break your life by what you think about yourself.

You are strong.

TONY'S LIST

DECEMBER 10, 2011

There's so much anticipation lurking around the holiday season. Tony has been on his best behavior and is following each and every tradition we've established over the years. We transformed our home into a winter wonderland the weekend after Thanksgiving, and the holiday music has not stopped playing throughout the house. At any given moment, I hear Tony singing Christmas songs, strolling through the house, and wearing his Santa hat. It's his favorite time of year.

There are many traditions in our families, but the biggest one is when we all gather at my parents' house for Christmas Eve. It's crowded and hot, even though the outside temperature is usually below zero, and it's very, very noisy. We spend weeks preparing Tony for the giant sleepover, which happens every single year.

"Are you ready for the noise?" I ask. "Are you ready for the very loud noises?" Tony always smiles with a little naughty laugh, responding, "Yes!"

But it isn't really that simple. There have been years when Dave and I were so bummed because Tony wanted nothing to do with our celebrations and years when we were very stressed out because Tony couldn't handle the commotion and the noise. For many years, Tony was disruptive; he'd break things or not wait his turn, take someone's toy, or scream for no reason. There were tears—many, many tears. Some would just pour out over a simple statement said quietly to me in the kitchen: "I don't know how you do it."

"I don't," I'd reply, and then I'd sneak away and sob.

There was yelling, fights about discipline, moments of sweating, and stress eating. You know, when you shovel things into your mouth without realizing it because you can't handle the stress. Seriously, it's not healthy.

Our families have been very patient. Then a few years ago, we got smart. I think this is about the time when we earned our "master's in autism," as I like to call it. We've had enough research and experience under our belt to call it a full blown master's degree in autism. A master's in learning how to be a proactive rather than a reactive parent, how to plan ahead, how to foresee challenges and cut them off at the pass, strategies for meltdowns or inappropriate questions, reinforcement for moments of greatness, etc…

With another degree in crisis management, anyone else familiar with this master's degree program? We got smart by giving Tony a job. Every Christmas Eve,

Tony is in charge of "the list." My parents' number the presents for the grandchildren under the tree, and my Mom keeps a master list. She hides it and then gives it only to Tony on the day before Christmas. He then memorizes it in a matter of seconds, and she puts it away. At gift opening time, she hands it back to Tony who uses it only as a reference and to cross off the numbers when they are opened.

It's a genius idea. He loves his job and takes it very seriously. The Santa hat is worn by the person whose name Tony calls from "the list." Everyone participates. Everyone follows the tradition, no matter what their age.

Another smart idea is to always designate one room that Tony can go to and close the door to use as his "quiet space." He usually spends a lot of time in there when the noise gets too loud or there's just too much stimulation. I've been known to utilize that room also. And, um, so has Grandpa. Like I said, we have incredibly supportive families.

And this year we'll start new traditions on my husband's side of the family since we lost both of his parents last year. Whatever we do, it will be fun to all be together and to hold on to their family traditions too. That's an even larger crowd in a much smaller space. But it's not a holiday sleepover, and Tony usually does very well, except for the year he and Grandpa Gene fought over the remote, that didn't go over so well with either of them. I think I know where Tony got his strong will from.

Ah, the holidays. Is everyone ready? Are you ready to continue all the family traditions? At least for our families, we know that the traditions will never be broken or forgotten as long as our Tony is around.

FOR MY BEAUTIFUL MOTHER

JANUARY 12, 2012

I received this letter from Tony one day after school when he was eighteen years old. It was hidden in his backpack. On the front of the envelope it said, "For my beautiful mother." It completely made my day, my week, my year. All we need are little reassurances that he's happy and content. Since he can't express that to me or anyone else, this was an extra magical moment.

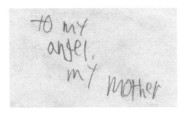

To my
angel,
my mother

Dear mom,
I would really lik
to go to Lake
Crystal. I have
had a great
week. It's
impossible. Soon?
Love your son
Tony

I love the random words "it's impossible. Soon?" I'm sure he's saying, "It's possible, yes? And soon?" Or even, "I'm possible," meaning that he's met the expectations. As his mom and translator, that would be my first guess. And how proud I was at this moment! Yes! Of course, I will take you! You have communicated a request to me in almost clear English. I've waited years and years for this! So yes, sweet man-boy, I will take you to your favorite place on earth. The little town nestled in the southern part of our state, hidden in the fields and lakes, yet so quiet and beautiful and full of our family's history. Love this guy.

The Decorations

MARCH 2, 2012

We had another *normal* breakthrough! Tony decorated his room! Now hold on, in our world, it's very big. It may not seem that way, but when you realize just how much we've struggled with simple conversation, you may get the picture. Anytime there's a small window into Tony's world, we are overwhelmed with joy in this house!

Since our oldest moved away to college three years prior to this event, Tony moved into his room and hasn't changed a thing. I'm sure he did that because he missed him so much, and sleeping in that room could freeze the change that was happening all around him during that time. It makes sense when you think of it that way, right? So, last week we had a doctor's appointment. If you can recall, any appointment is difficult for Tony. It has everything to do with changing the routine, the atmosphere of the office, the humming

of the lights, how much chaos is going on in the waiting room, whether a baby is crying in a one-mile radius,
etc. (See chapter "To The Mom in The Waiting Room"
for further explanation.)

My blood pressure was increasing rapidly. I could
feel my face flush and my heart start to palpitate. The
last time we visited this particular doctor, it was a total
disaster. It was a few days before his private high school
graduation party and anxiety was super high. The doctor switched the location on us at the last minute, and
let's just say it was our hardest appointment yet. (See
chapter "It Happened One Day" for yet another reference leading up to this appointment.)

Tony's violence and explosive language had everyone
in that office on edge and most of us in tears. But our
lives have changed dramatically since that appointment
as we've been able to stabilize his moods and behaviors through medication. I fought medication for years,
but it's truly changed our lives. So you can see why my
anxiety was high last week, I was anticipating the pos-
sibility of the same behaviors. He's so unpredictable.
And I was taking him alone this time.

I stopped at a gas station before our appointment and bought a Hollywood gossip teen magazine
for him. He loves anything Hollywood. I mean, he
is my child, after all. (See chapter "I'd Like to Thank
the Academy.") That was the best thing I could have
done. We got to the doctor's office, and I gave him the
magazine. He sat with his legs crossed, and read the
entire thing as we waited for over twenty minutes in a
very small, crowded room. He was fine. My heart was

beating out of my chest. They finally called his name, and he marched back to the room, participated in the conversation. Well, a little, but he was trying. And the appointment went off without a hitch. I was so proud of him! Could I have figured this simple strategy out years ago? Sure, but the mystery lies in that every age, every stage, brings new behaviors and challenges. This wouldn't have worked back a few years ago.

When we got home, he ran upstairs to his room. He usually goes into our room to be on his iPad, so this was unusual. I went about my business and then started to hear noises. *Kerplunk, kerplunk, kerplunk shuffle, shuffle, grunt.* An hour passed, and there was more noise. *Kerplunk, grunt.*

Oh boy, what is he breaking? I went to his door and knocked. "Hi, Tony! It's Mom. You okay?"

"Go away!" Tony shouts.

"Tone?" I say sternly, silently reminding him that is not an appropriate answer.

"The decorations," he says.

Oh! What? He's decorating his room? Excitement is in the air. "Can I see?" I ask ever so sweetly.

He opens the door. What I saw was just so incredibly wonderful. Just a little peek inside his mind! He had hung posters from magazines, organized all of his almanacs and VHS videos, hung a puppy calendar, *and* stacked his many, many books. I snapped a quick picture of just one side.

"Hey!" he yells. "I'm trying to get busy here!" It's another Tonyism, which means "leave me alone, please."

"I'm just so proud of you, Tony! I want a picture so I can remember," I answered.

"Fine." Always his go-to answer. That means he approves and has accepted your request.

I shut the door with a smile and ran to get the others so they could also witness it.

PS: Oh, and the *kerplunck* noise? Oh yeah, that was the stapler. He stapled all the posters to the walls and the back of his bedroom door. Oops! It sure is a good thing my husband spent years in construction. He can fix anything.

The eYebRow eRRoR

AUGUST 17, 2012

Around the time Tony turned fourteen years old, he developed some pretty serious facial hair. He was intrigued with his new look, and he checked himself out in the mirror quite often. My husband and I had discussed getting him an electric razor and hiding it so when Tony was ready, or more appropriately when we were ready, we'd be prepared. Well, that day came sooner than we'd expected.

A few years prior, I'd purchased a great social story-book called *Taking Care of Myself: A Healthy Hygiene, Puberty and Personal Curriculum for Young People with Autism* by Mary Wrobel. There are simple, direct, and easy-to-understand stories written for people who are visually strong yet cognitively weak. The curriculum was designed specifically to address the health and safety needs of students with autism spectrum disorder.

We had sticky notes, folded pages, and highlighted sections of this book and have used it again and again starting in middle school. One such highlighted and tagged section is called "Shaving My Face." I studied and read it with my husband, preparing for the day we'd venture up enough nerve to tackle this rite of passage with our Tony. Looking back, I'm pretty sure Tony read it too as it sat on my nightstand. It only takes one look, and he's got it saved in his memory card in his mind. It makes sense now.

A couple months later at Christmas, Grandma bought him an electric razor. He unwrapped it, and his eyes lit up. I should have taken that clue more seriously. He handed it to me, and I said I'd save it for when we were "ready." Looking back, here's another clue. The word *ready* has no meaning to him. There's no picture for it. And, well, I guess he was ready.

I hid the electric razor when we got home in my usual good hiding spot. Little did I know that I was the only one who thought it was a hiding spot. The next day, I was working in my office, and Tony came down, burst in, and said "Hello, Mommy!" He obviously wanted me to look at him. These moments don't come often, so I was excited to oblige. I turned to look and gasped, holding my hands over my mouth. *What happened? What is wrong with his face?* I thought to myself.

Because of the way I reacted, even though no words were expressed, Tony was severely disappointed and started frowning. "Oh *no!*" he screamed as he truly saw the horror in my face—which, I have to admit, was a wonderful step in progress toward reading people's expression, so hooray for that! Once I gained my composure, I stood up and realized just what was freaking me out so badly. Tony had shaved his face. But not just his face. He had also shaved his eyebrows, sideburns, and forehead. It was an odd look. A really, really odd look. I think at first I thought something had happened to his eyes. They looked swollen or sunken or something different. I learned many years ago that your eyebrows are to your eye what your hair is to your face—a frame. Now I clearly see why that makes sense.

As I stood to give my man-boy a hug and assured him that he did a terrific job, I told him that he looked very, very handsome. I grabbed his cheeks and said, "Who is so handsome?"

"Me am," he replied, something we've said to each other in the mirror for years after getting ready in the morning. I've done it with all my boys. Just a mom thing. I talked to him about safety and about not shaving again until his dad or I could help him. He agreed, mostly because I think he was still upset with my reaction. I touched his eyebrows while we were looking in the mirror together, and he said, "Oh *no*! Do again. Put back?"

I chuckled. "It's okay, Tony. Mom can draw them on with my special pencil until they grow back. And they will grow back because remember, hair grows, right? It's okay. I think you look very handsome, and I'm so very proud of you."

"Proud," he adds. I guess he was proud too.

So for the next few weeks, I patiently drew his eyebrows on every morning with my eyebrow pencil. I warned his team at school of the new look, just so none of them had the same reaction I did. One must always plan ahead in this house. So the moral of this story is this: don't buy the electric razor until you are ready to shave that very same day, if your child is like mine. Hide your razor blades, and you'll be fine. Oh, and one more thing: rethink your hiding places. I think they are on to us.

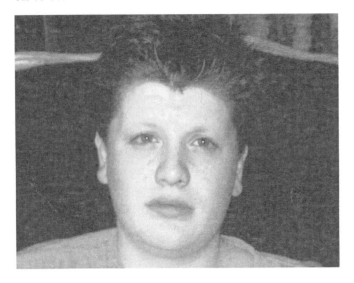

The CONVERSATION

AUGUST 14, 2012

I'm gonna be honest with you. This autism thing is exhausting at times. In fact, often. For seventeen years, I feel we've been researching, seeking, questioning, and even arguing at times over what's best for our Tony. It's a constant fight to pull my Tony from the comfort of his world and pull him into ours. Sometimes, I wonder why I even try. But then there's times like this that make it all worthwhile.

A few weeks ago, my younger son was having his buddies sleep over. I mentioned to Tony that the guys were coming over to stay, and they would be hanging downstairs. Tony was quick to reply, "What about *my* friends? I like sleepovers!" My heart ached. "I know, Tony. And I'm so proud of you. We will plan a special sleepover for Tony's friends, okay? We will do that very soon."

"Who?" he replied, which really means "when." He still has trouble with "WH" questions.

"We'll check the calendar tomorrow, okay?" I answered.

"But who?" he continued. And I know where that was going. We could play that game for hours. I gently kissed his forehead and said good night. I turned to leave as the tears poured down my cheeks.

"Good night, Mommy! Check the calendar," he added.

I closed the door. I couldn't help my tears. My son is nineteen years old and has yet to know the reality of a sleepover with friends. Does he realize that he doesn't really have any friends his own age? Outside of his cousins, there really isn't anyone else his age. Yes, there are some from his school program, but we have never had them over to play, hang, or even visit. I don't think they are independent enough either.

It's okay, right? I mean, cousins are usually your first and lifelong friends, right? There's nothing wrong with that. That's not what I'm saying. I think it's just becoming perfectly clear just how alone Tony is the older he gets. And quite frankly, that thought scares me to death.

I decided to go back in his room to check on him. There he was, on his iPad, watching a show in another language. Happy as can be. I sat down on the bed next to him.

"What are you watching, Tony?"

Silence. "Go away!" he grumbled.

"Tony, I want to talk to you. Can you look into my eyes for a minute?" I asked.

He gave me a quick glance and then looked away. I know I had his attention for an entire second.

"Tony, do you want to live with friends someday, away from home, just like your big brother did?" I asked, holding my breath.

"Yes," he said, no hesitation.

"That's great, honey! Can you look into my eyes again? You know, it will take you a little longer to be living with friends because you have autism. You know that, right?" I whispered.

He looked deep into my eyes and frowned. "It's hard," he responds.

"I know it is, honey." I gasped. "But it's not your fault. And it's not my fault or Dad's fault either. It's just...hard."

"Hard," he said again, adding some inappropriate swear words, or appropriate, depending on how you look at it.

Yes, I think. That's putting it mildly, Tony.

"I am so, so sorry, Tony. I really am. But would you like to stay with Mom and Dad until you're ready to live with friends?" I asked.

"Yes. Sorry too. Good-bye now. You can leave now!" he said, his voice getting louder.

We have been literally choking under the pressure—financially, emotionally, physically—to get him where he needs to be. And yes, it's exhausting. But guess what? It's exhilarating too. It's the most incredible, fulfilling feeling when I can converse with my son after all these years. That conversation went back and forth ten times! And it's taken us over seventeen years to get to this point! Through my tears, my husband and I clapped, smiled, and even giggled because everything he said was appropriate—even the swear words. I don't blame him! Sometimes I'd love to let a few of them slip too.

The sermon at church the following Sunday was this: Suffering has become a real means for grace. We must learn to pick up our cross for the grace to flow. Pick up your cross, and bear it! Do not drag your cross, but accept it. Accept your suffering, and use it; use it to help heal others.

And with that, a shiver went up and down my spine. Something awakened inside me. This has been such a gift to our family, this autism. I know that may sound funny. But for someone who pretty much lived for herself up to the point of having children and realizing this diagnosis, she has now learned to live for others. For someone who was a social butterfly and dreamed of traveling the world, she has evolved into a compassionate caretaker who dreams of helping others. The same goes for my husband. Watching him evolve has been amazing over the years. And this didn't happen overnight. In fact, we're still thick in the trenches. But now, we find ourselves asking, who can we help? Who else is struggling with these emotions, who else needs to pick up their cross?

In order to take care of others, you must first take care of yourself. We all know that. So don't forget it. Don't let that slip away because for many years, I did. And by the way, you have to be in pretty darn good shape to carry an actual cross, right?

SNeaKY LiTTLe gUY

AUGUST 22, 2012

Having a conversation with my neighbors the other night around the bonfire reminded me of a time when Tony was younger. We always hired boy babysitters during his late elementary school years because he was so active, and they could keep up with him. One such babysitter was our neighbor who was about four years older than Tony. He was a great babysitter, very hands-on. I mean, he'd get down and actually play in the mud with Tony on a few occasions. He would play make-believe, even though Tony couldn't talk back and forth, and act out scenes with him. They'd play with cars, animated figures, create forts, and do all kinds of things like that. One night, my little stinker was on a mischievous roll, and he decided to grab the scissors and cut a huge chunk of hair out of his own head. It was large enough to leave a noticeable hole. I was so thankful that it was Tony's head and not the babysitter's! Later, the babysitter said, "But I just turned my head for a second! Really!"

That's our life with Tony. Not to worry, I assured the babysitter, "This is not our first rodeo. It happens frequently around here. That's why you'll notice all the scissors are hidden." Later that night, I recall, Tony locked that same babysitter out of the house. The babysitter's parents, who are great friends of ours, had to come over, knock on the back sliding doors, and try to coax Tony into letting them in. I believe he teased them for a while and was running around giggling, saying, "No!" Oh boy, that poor babysitter. That's life with our Tone.

One other moment comes to mind when Tony was about five years old. We had toys scattered all over the family room. I believe his speech therapist and occupational therapist had just left. He was pretty wound up, but he sat playing with a magnetic alphabet toy. I remember how hard we worked on letter recognition. It was winter, so we had holiday music and our gas fireplace on. I was in the kitchen and could see him through the railing. He was singing and playing, so I thought I had a few minutes to clean up and maybe start baking, which I did often because the boys liked to participate. All of a sudden I smelled something. Something's burning! But it's an unusual smell. I looked around the entire house and even called my husband. Frantically, I ran through the house yelling, "Hey guys! What is that smell?" My other two boys shrugged their shoulders and continued about their business. Tony started giggling. I knew that was trouble. I finally turned to the gas fireplace and saw a rainbow of melted magnetic letters running down the front glass. Tony had ever so quietly and secretly stuffed his alphabet letters down a tiny tilted opening in the front of the fireplace and joyfully watched them melt. It took us weeks to clean that up. Again, that's life with our Toneman. The little stinker, devilish grin and all.

WANTED: Things That Make Bubbles

AUGUST 24, 2012

Okay. What is going on? Is it a full moon? Lunar eclipse? Seasons changing? Did Tony eat something with a ton of gluten? Or is he just being a toddler again? The reason I'm asking is that lately, he cannot get enough of bubbles. He's experimenting with our three-cornered tub and turning on the jets, creating all kinds of mysterious bubbles. Bubbles everywhere. So much so that they are seeping out of the bathroom door. Yes, we had turned off the switch on several occasions so the jets no longer work. But please forgive me, I wanted to indulge in a lovely, relaxing bath the other night and forgot to turn them back off. Oops.

So far this week, he's used the following liquids to create bubbles, bubbles of any kind, before I could even get more bubble bath:

1. My favorite triple-milled glycerin bar—soap that is far too lathery to call it soap.

2. All of my shampoo. Yep, the good kind.

3. Every travel bottle of shampoo that we've accumulated over the years, found in a drawer.

4. Dish soap. Yep. The whole bottle. And guess what? It's concentrated. So that make *triple* the amount of suds. Triple!

5. Dishwasher detergent. This didn't bubble as well, so hopefully will not be a repeat offender.

6. Window cleaner.

7. Shower spray for hard-water stains, the entire bottle.

8. Tub and tile bathroom cleaner. Again, it's concentrated. Makes major bubbles. It was a huge hit.

9. All-purpose cleaner.

10. My facial cleanser. Yep. All of it.

11. Toothpaste.

12. Lotion. Any kind. I'm sure he figured out that wasn't a huge success in the bubble department.

13. Eye makeup remover.

14. And finally, laundry soap.

And these are only the things I've been able to figure out! I kept noticing things missing, saying to myself, "I could have sworn I had a brand new bottle of _____."

Did I mention he still drinks the bathwater? Oh, and that he's nineteen? Yep. He's been quite the scientist this week. So before you throw out any liquids that are nontoxic, free of harmful chemicals, and can create massive bubbles, please think about donating them to the *Tony Scientific Research Fund*. All donations accepted. Results not guaranteed. No documentation will be supplied. Just some good old-fashioned fun. Oh, and some water damage to the bathroom too, but who's counting?

eaRLY iNTeRVeNTioN

AUGUST 28, 2012

Early intervention—we all know what that means. I'm not going to talk about early intervention therapy. I'm going to talk about the way I intervened early in our autism days. I have an apology to make.

Back when Tony was younger, I think around the time he was six or seven, we were on our way to a resort up north. We'd been going to this same resort since I was a young child, the same week every year. It was a huge family tradition on my side of the family, which Tony loved. It was often very hard for him, but he loved it. We were all squished into a cabin without air conditioning and barely a kitchen; but it had a lake front view, and the sun set across the lake every night. It was pure heaven. And it was just family, every year for an entire week. No phones, no TVs (well, there was one from the 1970s with one local channel for weather updates)—no electronics of any kind were allowed. All his cousins were there, which were literally all of his friends. We all loved it!

Back to my apology.

We had to cut the long drive in half, so we stopped at a McDonald's along the way and met up with Tony's Aunt Libby. We were eating lunch outside, and I noticed out of the corner of my eye that another family with small children had set up their lunch just a couple of tables away. Tony was very loud and animated, as he was most of the time back then—oh, who am I kidding, he still is. He was singing, flapping his hands in large, overexaggerated motions, and climbing all over the play area. All of a sudden, I see Tony approaching the family, and before I could get up and fly over to intervene, he had grabbed a huge handful of their french fries and ran away.

I remember hearing gasps and sharp comments about lack of discipline and lots of bickering from the other mom. "What a little brat! Who does that? What's wrong with him?" The dad said nothing and kept his head low. I thought Aunt Libby and my husband were going to snap at any moment. They were steaming and wanted to scream back at the other mom. I love family. Yeah! Go beat her up, the big bully.

But they refrained. Trembling, I quickly got up from my chair and went over to apologize. But as I was about to speak, the other mom said, "You should control your child!" I gulped. And completely changed what I was going to say in a split second.

"You're right. You're right. And I'm trying. I'm really trying. You see, my son has autism, and it's a very complicated, exhausting, and humbling experience. I'm very sorry that he ate your French fries, and I will buy you another pack of fries. At this point, my son is unable to control his behaviors, but we are working very hard with him. And also"—I looked deep into her eyes with my glossy, teary eyes, from one mom to another—"if you could refrain from any other comments about our parenting, I would really appreciate it. I heard every word."

I thought the other mom's face was going to burst because she was turning many shades of purple, past red, to purple.

Yeah, I heard you. And I called you out. All I remember is the dad saying, "That won't be necessary. We don't need any more fries. I'm so sorry." And they packed up and left.

I wasn't looking for an apology. In fact, I wanted to apologize to them. Yes, what he did was inappropriate. But what *she* did was ignorant. And I was really shocked at how calmly I handled it.

I think if I remember correctly, I was just completely exhausted and just didn't have it in me to fight. I wanted to apologize for the intrusion and the lack of social skills on my child's behalf. But more importantly, I wanted to educate. And I started that day. One person at a time. Autism and discipline are both difficult things to navigate. Put them together and it's nearly impossible. Nearly impossible, meaning it is possible, it just takes an extreme amount of patience and time.

So the next time you feel like someone else is watching, judging, or criticizing you and/or your child, take a step back and breathe before you respond. Try to educate, not just defend your child's behaviors. Because all of us know just how difficult it is to control behaviors, those behaviors of our children and the judgment of others.

a BOY aND HiS DOG

AUGUST 29, 2012

Poor naughty little Beau. Well, little, no. Naughty, yes.
But more patient than any human could ever be.

Tony and Beau have a unique bond. I really had
my doubts when we first started talking about getting
a dog all those years ago (see previous chapter for a
refresher on how we decided on and found Beau). But
from the minute we brought Beau home (pronounced
as Bo, Tony added the French spelling), he has somehow managed to tackle and understand this autism
thing—almost better than us sometimes.

I get it—animals have this unique ability to sense
those in need to comfort, to calm, and to love uncondi-
tionally. I think everyone should own a dog. I really do.
And I remember specifically saying that I would never
get another dog because it's just heartbreaking when
you lose them. Only now, I couldn't imagine our family
without this dog.

Beau has put up with some serious hard play, which we knew he would endure, having three boys in the house and our friend autism. That's why we specifically picked out the chubbiest and the naughtiest dog of the bunch. The breeder told us he'd be a big boy. And he wasn't lying. Beau is about 114 lbs of pure chubby muscle. Although lately, he's on a diet because we don't want to shorten his life or have him suffer from joint problems. So he's on a diet regimen, and he's a little grumpy about it. Welcome to the club, chublets. We are all limiting our calories these days.

The other day I caught Tony trimming Beau's nails. Poor Beau just lay there, not putting up a fight, and let Tony meticulously trim his nails, pick his nails, and yes, file his nails. I love how intense Tony was, concentrating on getting all of Beau's nails smooth and level. Seriously, that's some patient dog.

As I said in my earlier chapter, Beau is another set of eyes for us to help watch Tony. He has a special bark when Tony has left the house. And when Tony goes outside, Beau will jump up on the couch and look out the window, watching to make sure he's safe. And if Tony is wandering, he will alert me. I love that. Wherever Tony is, Beau is not far away.

Beau is also gluten-free. Well, by default. He gets to eat all the spilled food, which is quite a bit, but we are working on our table manners, or the "pretend" spilled food since Tony is quite the sharer, and he occasionally has been spotted sharing the popcorn bowl.

Beau's a helper at bedtime. He'll jump up to say good night and lie on Tony's feet to help calm him.

That always makes Tony smile. If for some reason Tony does not want to be disrupted or doesn't want someone in his room, we can always bring Beau as our negotiator. Works every time.

Beau has been known to stir the pot on few occasions. And by that I mean he starts making trouble, causing chaos. Tony is always first to participate. It always brings Tony out of a bad mood or an anxious moment. I'm sure Beau senses that. So together, the two toddlers are a handful—Beau and Tony, I mean. They are always up to something, whether that's chasing each other through the house or drawing with sidewalk chalk.

Tony loves to get Beau to do the naughty run. This is where Beau tucks his big rump in and runs like a crazy man outside or inside. It's the funniest thing in the world to watch a dog of that size try to sprint around a dining room table without breaking anything. Seriously, it makes us smile while yelling to get him out of the house.

But he never fails us when we need him, or when Tony needs him. He protects the door that Tony is behind during a tough episode. Oh, Beau. You're such a stinker. But you're also an angel. You've become much more than just a pet. You're a brother, a speech therapist, an occupational therapist, a weighted blanket, a parent, and a friend—all wrapped up into one big, white, furry, hug machine. Who would have known?

HeY, WaiT a MiNUTe, MR. POSTMAN

SEPTEMBER 10, 2012

Dear Mr. Postman,

Please deliver something. Anything. I've been just standing here waiting…for a card or just a magazine or maybe a Netflix DVD…or any surprise to this address. Coupons will work. Packages are better.

Love, Tony

I don't think the mailman has any idea just how important he is in our lives. I don't think he knows the anticipation and the angst that comes daily upon his arrival. I'm sure he has no idea that any delay in delivering the mail could set us back for weeks. And I'm positive that he doesn't realize that we have the National Postal

Holidays posted in our kitchen, so we are well aware of the "no mail days" throughout the year.

I've tried introducing Tony to the current mailman, but in our area the mail is outsourced, and there is rarely the same delivery man. Hopefully that will change. I would love to have that personal relationship with our mail carrier like we did when Tony was younger. Heck, we'd even make him or her some fabulous treats!

Tony has a couple of pen pals (thank you, Grandma and her good friends), and he loves getting letters. Although he's only responded with pictures and paintings, we are working on letter writing. I truly believe it's a lost art, and I'd love to see him write a nice, long letter. We'll get there someday. But currently, he is not cooperating with this form of communication.

There's just no substitute for physical mail. Since Tony isn't on e-mail yet (which I believe is a very good thing at this time) or Facebook, Twitter, or even Pinterest, this is his social media, the mail. He's started to communicate with the outside world through mail. He fills out every single card that falls out of any magazine, which explains the abundance of magazines arriving weekly. I don't always catch him as he sneaks out to the mailbox; and quite frankly, it humors me that he would try to sneak a subscription to Rolling Stone or Conde Nast Traveler. He fills the cards out so nicely; his name, address, zip-code, and my e-mail address. Do you know how long we've been working on that goal, the goal of writing his name and address and then to add an e-mail address? Bravo!

Knowing our Tony has no limits, we've invited him to subscribe to four magazines: *People, OK Magazine, Rolling Stone*, and *Conde Nast Traveler*. But I see that the *Smithsonian* and *Harper's Magazine* have started arriving. Seems I missed those subscription cards.

But how can I limit his library of knowledge? He's getting a healthy dose of Hollywood gossip, rock and roll, and amazing travel destinations. When I googled the *Smithsonian Magazine*, it explained that it was created to stir curiosity in already receptive minds, and it would deal with history as it is relevant to the present, which is right up Tony's alley. And *Harper's* was described as a monthly magazine of literature, politics, culture, finance, and the arts. Okay. I can see that.

So each day, just after lunch, when he arrives home from school, Tony will start pacing outside waiting for the mail. Sometimes, he will sit in the glider and sing, but on tougher days he'll pace, wander, swear, and peel anything he can find, such as a tree, or black vinyl fencing, the deck paint, etc.

The day after Labor Day this year, he waited for three hours in the hot sun, which also means I waited because he wanders. So for our neighbors' sake, I waited too. And we also know that on Mondays, the mail arrives later than normal, so we plan accordingly.

But just as fast as a bad mood may come, it disappears as we hear the hum of the mail truck coming up the road. It's very exciting. Some kids get excited for the ice cream truck. But not my man-boy. He digs the mail truck.

The iNVENTORY

SEPTEMBER 27, 2012

For years now, Tony has been compiling lists. Lists of all kinds. There are piles of printed lists in his room—episode lists from Disney shows, movies, Sesame Street, Dora, the Muppets, the Garfield Show, Barney, and our entire Netflix rental history—week by week since 2004. Lots and lots of lists. Lots and lots of paper. I know it's important to him. It's his inventory, something he can physically touch, see, and read whenever he wants.

His latest list-making task is taking inventory of all the VHS tapes in his possession, including those at Grandma's, which I'm sure he's claimed as his own.

His categories are the following, to name just a few:

- 20th Century Fox Selections
- United Artists
- Paramount Pictures (seems to be a favorite because there are four pages here)

- Columbia Tristar
- Warner Bros. (another favorite spouting four pages)
- Universal
- Dreamworks
- Hollywood Miramax Touchstone Pictures
- CBS/FOX
- Touchstone Buena Vista
- MGM/UA

Nineteen pages total, so far. Small print. Color coded.

Now I'm not sure if these are all in his possession, or if they are a complete list and he's trying to complete his list by purchasing them all. Not sure. May never know. But he's finding some fantastic deals at thrift stores, and he previews each one. If they do not work, he dismembers them, throws them away, and continues his search. I just wish he could tell us what he's looking for because we'd all help. But that's the struggle, he doesn't answer my questions. Can't or won't, I'm just not sure. He sure keeps us guessing. But in the meantime, it is so intriguing to watch him in progress. He's intently writing, sorting, hunting, and categorizing. Have I mentioned how much we struggle to get him to *write*?

That's why this seems like a small miracle in this house. And that's why I had to share it with you all. This is simply amazing. It's another look into his mind, his world. And it fascinates us.

We love his guy so much, and we aren't always welcomed into his world. So you can imagine how much this makes us smile. And you can imagine why I continue to buy paper, printer ink, clipboards, markers, and staples. Whatever it takes to be invited in.

WHY WE HIDE THE MATCHES

SEPTEMBER 29, 2012

There's a small fascination with fire in our house, mostly bonfires and candles. It started a few years ago when Tony showed an interest in cooking. One day, he was toasting some bread, and he laid the dish towel on top of the toaster. Lo and behold, a small fire. He quickly threw it in the sink and ran water over it before I could race up the stairs because I could smell the smoke. And I'm always on the lookout for that smell.

He then started lighting candles over and over and watching them burn. I could sense his growing interest and was overly cautious at all times, but he still would sneak in a little paper burn here and there, holding it carefully over the flames; thus, ended my candle burning in the house. Bummer. We had just gotten past the toddler stage of no candle burning, and now I had to give them up again. Oh well. There are worse things.

Thank goodness for battery operated and remote candles that are now available. Someone's ingenious idea!

So ever since then, we've been very careful and have always hidden the matches and fire starters outside, where he'd never find them. Until one day he did.

Dave was out of town and Tony had come home from school quite agitated and aggressive. I could tell it was going to be a tough afternoon. So I shut down my computer, stopped working, and surrendered to our friend, Mr. Autism. Thank goodness, I did. Because in the short time I finished in my office, Tony had already started a bonfire outside. A. Huge. Bonfire.

He had stacked the wood in a tepee style, just as he's seen his dad do many times, stuffed some "things" underneath as kindling, the likes of which were never identified, and lit it all on fire.

He was pacing, chanting, swearing, and still quite aggressive. I could tell that he was not going to talk to me or that I was not going to be able to intervene. I could smell some odd things burning, and later discovered that he had burned the shirt off his back, one tennis shoe, a plastic glass, a football, a small figurine toy of The Hulk, a spoon, a pencil, and those are only the things I could identify. Who knows what else made it in there?

It scared me, and it was quickly getting out of control, so I did the best thing I knew how to do. I joined him. And later, so did his little brother. For the next four hours, he threw every log on the fire; and I taught him, silently, about fire safety. We sat around the bonfire and enjoyed his creation. I must admit, it was quite peaceful. Words were barely spoken, and we all were very relaxed and ready for bed by the time the last log burned out. And that was the end of his fire obsession. We still have bonfires, and he watches us entertain around our bonfire pit or at the neighbor's, so he knows it's a social activity. I really do believe that I had to just give in and let him build a bonfire in order for him to fulfill his obsession at the time. So, we did it in a safe environment and with silent instruction. Even though I was nervous, I'm glad we did it and got it out of his system. Oh, we'll still hide the matches, and I highly suggest you do too. Simply because one can never be too cautious when our friend, Mr. Autism, is around.

CAN YOU CUT THE HAIR?

OCTOBER 12, 2012

Breakthrough moment today! Tony *asked* me to cut his hair. If you remember correctly, communicating through questions is not an easy thing for him to do. We've worked very hard for many, many years on this. However, today he voiced what his mind was thinking. He asked me to cut his hair! Thinking back to many other episodes of hair cutting this always brings anxiety to this house. We used to take Tony to a children's hair salon, then a local barber, then a discount chain, which ended in disaster (see previous chapter), then a local gal who cut hair in her home. She was the best, and we were with her through his preteen/teenage years. But as hormones would have it, he got a little too comfortable and was overly friendly. He even started roaming through her house and personal belongings, so I needed to find a better alternative. Then I finally got smart. Well, my oldest son got smart. "Mom? Why aren't you just using a number two or three on him?" he said. "That's all I use. College kids can't afford haircuts." Like seriously. And Tony clearly was in college now, he's always referring to his transitional program as "County College," so much so that the staff now refers to it that way too.

Okay. So we bought a really nice hair trimming set and started to cut his hair on our own. It's not rocket science. But sometimes, the obvious still needs to be pointed out. So between shaving and haircuts, there's a lot of hair that needs to be cleaned up. He's blessed with an abundance of hair, which just cracks me up because as his summer buzz cuts grow out, he starts to resemble a Smurf or even a Chia Pet. Not a good look for a college kid. This is now the perfect situation because his hair looks nice, doesn't need to be combed, and is easy to clean in the shower. I think I'll start calendaring haircuts so he knows when to expect them. And another thought, where to hide the hair trimmer set so there's no more hair disasters. I hid it so well last time that even I couldn't find it.

Hmmm. What's the worst thing that could happen if he finds it and cuts his own hair?

At least I can count on one thing: his hair grows really, really fast.

KNOW YOUR BOUNDARIES

OCTOBER 11, 2012

There's been a lot of talk in the media lately about autism and wandering issues. It's brought back a ton of memories, so much so that I can really appreciate how far we've come. My sister-in-law, Jess, reminded me of an e-mail I sent to the family back when we were in the trenches of the wandering stage and the phobia stage.

Let me give you a little background. We were dealing with his dog phobia where he wouldn't go outside in either the front or backyard, ever. There were dogs surrounding us, happy, large and small, lovely dogs that wouldn't hurt a flea. But for some reason, his fear grew into a deep phobia. We worked intensely with a behavioral therapist to get the dog who quickly became the love of his life.

Getting our fence was just part of that process. We just could not get Tony to go outside to play, and it was heartbreaking. With our fence and fence doors that also could be locked, we added a security system and switched to keyed locks, so we could hide or carry the keys. It's much better now, but there were years when I slept with one eye open at all times. We have wonderful neighbors and now a large dog that really help us keep track of him.

So the e-mail read like this (notice the jubilant overtone with all those exclamation points):

May 21, 2007 9:06 p.m.

The Becker's had a very triumphant day today! Tony played outside in his own yard from the minute he got home from school at 2:20 p.m. until just now—9pm! We had our fence installed today! I walked the yard with Tony and showed him how secure it was and how tall it is. He tested out the gates to make sure they were closed tightly, and saw the locks. He smiled and said, "This is great!" I got a big hug and off he went to the swing set. I must say, it's been over 2 years and he's totally grown out of the swings! I guess I'll need to find some adult size swings for him. :-)

We also put up the out-of-ground pool (a Tony donation from some good friends!), and even though it was freezing cold water, Tony played in it for over 3 hours! I think it will be a hit!

It's easy to take simple things like this for granted…but in our house, today was a banner day! It's going to be great for Tony to feel safe in his own backyard again.

Onward and upward! On to the next challenge! Bring it on!!

Becki

Even though our son is now nineteen years old, he still cannot be left alone for safety reasons. Ever. At least not now. Still. But we're hoping someday that will change. My advice to those families with younger children going through these same issues? Record it. Embrace it. Find the good in your situation. Because some day, I sincerely promise, some day it will all make sense.

change

JANUARY 22, 2013

Sometimes it's very difficult to share things that are so real, so raw, so personal. But all it takes is a comment from another parent, a fellow blogger, an old friend, or a beloved family member to put it right back into perspective.

We had a wonderful holiday—one of the best that I can remember. It was full of family, food, and celebration. Tony did phenomenal—he really did. There were a few, minor exceptions, but overall I was so happy with how he handled the chaos and the noise. He loves Christmas and all things family. He was more present and in the moment than ever before.

January is always a month to regroup, clean up, set goals, and start implementation. Such is the case in our house. We are in "operation room change." My youngest is moving his room downstairs, which was home to my office for almost eighteen years. Let's just say that there's a lot of *stuff* in there. Sorting through art, school projects, tax info, work papers, training notes…it's been quite a reflective month. I had to laugh so many times as I stumbled upon a piece of artwork or a painting. I clearly remember my oldest son screaming at the top of his lungs when he was about five years old, "Don't throw that away! That's my whole life so far!" (referring to a bag of art that I was going to recycle). And so I did not throw it away.

Fast forward to today. It's still here. And so are all of his sibling's creations. I still don't have the heart to throw them out.

So as my youngest is successfully transitioned into his new digs, we move on to Tony's room. Hmmm… What can I say? He's bursting at the seams as far as space is concerned. Tony is moving into the room my youngest just abandoned. It is now perfectly clean, with fresh paint, and new carpet is arriving next week. More space. A clean canvas. Tony will be able to move his entire VHS collection, along with his DVDs and *all* of his books, posters, and piles of episode lists (for an explanation of what that is, see chapter: The Inventory).

But not so fast! As you can imagine, all this change is taking a toll on Tony. Heightened anxiety comes with any change. He's had some moments—moments of anger and angst as he lets go of the *norm* and accepts the change.

He chose the paint color for his new room—same as his brother—Notre Dame gold. (Loves all things Irish!) As he waits for the new carpet, he's introducing himself to his new space by lying on the floor with the dog, reading, singing, inspecting Dad's painting job to great detail, and even dancing in the room.

We are trying to involve him as much as possible, and he even helped paint a wall. He was happy to cover the loud purple color left by his younger brother.

Meanwhile, my office is sprawled over two or three rooms. Oh, the sacrifices we make, right? At least my computer is working again. That is crucial. I felt like I was cut off from the world. Okay. Maybe not that dramatic—but close.

Those of us living with ASD (autism spectrum disorders) quickly learn that change is bad. Change is hard. Change is unwelcome. But then we quickly learn that change is inevitable. And we have to be brave and push the limits sometimes to be able to teach our kiddos that change will happen, and this is how we will do it together.

So as we move into the new year and create the *space* that we are seeking, I invite you to push the limits, even if ever so slightly. Make *this* year the year you got brave. Stretch. You'll be so thankful you did.

MORE TONYISMS

JANUARY 26, 2013

A couple of nights ago, Tony and I had a long discussion on healthy habits, like eating well, cutting back on pizzas, and exercising to help maintain a healthy weight. I mentioned a goal weight—not too hard—and gave him ideas to help lower the number on the scale, like certain exercises and sneaking less snacks. I was very careful in the words I chose, knowing he is very literal. But I gave up after a while, assuming he wasn't listening because he was singing, rocking, and he asked me to leave the room ever so politely.

So yesterday morning, exactly fifteen minutes before the school bus was to come, I caught Tony putting on his shoes.

"Hold on there, Buster! It's cold and snowy out. You'll want to wear your boots today," I said.

"'Buster?'" he asked.

"I mean Tony. I was talking to you, Tony," I replied.

"But I want the shoes!" he yelled.

And down he ran to the treadmill.

He ramped up the treadmill and started running. Huffing and puffing he ran, stopped, and ran again.

After ten minutes, he turned it off and ran up the stairs and into my bathroom.

All of a sudden, I heard him yell some not so appropriate words and scream "*What?*"

"*Excuse* me?" I say, running up the stairs. "We do not swear in this house!"

"The number's the same! Scale's broken. That's it. I'm done!" he bluntly reported.

And he marched down to the kitchen and grabbed a peppermint patty.

I feel your pain, buddy. I feel your pain. I just knew there was something wrong with that scale.

TiNY FOOTPRiNTS

JANUARY 31, 2013

If you recall, we are making some big changes in our house this month. The boys are changing rooms, and it's been quite an ordeal. While my husband was ripping up some old carpeting in my office (which is now my younger son's room), he found something remarkable.

A flashback in time.

Tiny little footprints on the concrete floor...

When I saw this, the memories came flooding back.

It was 1996, and I had just landed a job working from home. That was quite a big deal back then—at least in my area of the Midwest. It was the perfect fit. I could work remotely from home answering incoming calls that seemed as if I was in the big, downtown office (I worked in the travel industry at the time). I was thrilled! We were about a year and a half into the autism diagnosis, still quite in denial. But this was perfect. It would allow me to be home for all the therapies and appointments, yet still hold down a job.

So while my ever-so-talented husband was building my new office, my oldest son would be completely mesmerized and would put on a little tool belt and play "construction." My Tony—then nonverbal—would participate as well.

He, however, was a fast little sneak—a silent tornado, a master mess-maker.

We couldn't turn our backs for a minute back then, because Tony would always be into something. He was quick, he screamed all the time—even when he was happy, and he wasn't satisfied until he made a mess.

This day was no exception.

Dave was priming and taping the walls in my soon-to-be new office and walked away for a second—just a second.

Big mistake. *Big.*

When he returned he found Tony covered in white paint. Paint was dripping from the closet walls, and the cement floor was covered in paint blotches.

The work of an artist. Hmmm… Yes… If only we had seen it that way back then.

This was about that same time that Tony threw all of our very important diagnosis and IEP documents into the tub, soaking all the information that was yet so new to us. Panicked, I quickly laid all 200 pages out to dry. They are still crunchy, and I love it, because I remember how Tony giggled and giggled as I was grabbing the papers out of the tub. Stinker. I'm sure he got a time out or some form of punishment, which I'm also sure meant nothing to him at the time.

But we didn't know that.

And he always won my heart back before the next adventure began.

Leaving tiny footprints and big messes that we now can only treasure, my Toneman once again made us smile all these years later.

And now it's just a memory under some plush new carpeting, but it makes me smile every time I step into that room.

"The Phone Ring!"

MAY 9, 2013

Who keeps calling? Our phone is ringing off the hook! And every time it rings, Tony yells, "The phone ring!" (As if he needs to announce it.)

I'll tell you who's calling. And it cracks me up every time.

Tony's been a busy guy. I think he must be answering ads online. Seriously! I usually don't answer our landline phone (yes, we still have one) because everyone has our cell phone numbers. But lately it's gone wild, and I just had to investigate.

One call I answered the other morning went like this:

"Hello! May I speak to Tony?"

Stumbling, I say, "This is his mom?" Click. Wrong answer.

Next time I got smarter.

"Hello, is Tony in?" asks the unsuspecting caller.

"This is Tony," I say.

"Well, hello, Tony! This is _____ from _____ college. We understand you are interested in pursuing a career in criminal justice?" asks the soon-to-be-laughing caller.

I clear my throat. *Oh boy. What stage have we entered here?*

After explaining our situation and explaining the fact that Tony isn't actually interested in going off to their university, we have a sincere laugh together. I explain that this is a new skill and although I'm sorry for a false lead, I'm elated that he actually responded to something of interest, even though we're not sure if it was a flashy AD, a comic, or the actual words that caught his attention. Whatever the case, I politely ask to have our number removed from their system.

We'll see if that happens.

Later that same day…

"The phone ring!" yells Tony from his room.

"Okay. I got it!" I assure him. "Hello?" I so innocently ask.

"Hello! May I speak to Tony?" asks a young telemarketer.

"This is Tony," I say, smiling as I look over at my husband.

"Oh, hi, Tony! I'm calling to ask you if you're still interested in earning a supplemental income from home?" says the ever-so-un-expecting-hopeful-lead-purchaser.

Hmmm…I'm going to have to have a conversation with Tony about clicking on ads and giving out our personal information. Really? This? After all these years of working on him learning his contact information in the event of an emergency, we now have to tell him not to give it out?

His computer is not a "stranger" to him. He trusts it. How are we going to tackle this one? It seriously could be an issue. Oh, my…

Just another day in our household. Carry on, everyone.

And please, don't call our landline. Unless, of course, Tony asked you to.

The NexT chapTeR

When you have valuable information, it's important to share it with those you love and care about.

Our son Tony, who is now twenty years old, was diagnosed with autism at age two. Autism is a developmental disability that impacts normal development of the brain in the area of social interaction and communication skills. Autism is a difficult thing to understand. Doctors and experts still do not know everything there is to know. Yet, as a parent of an autistic child, that's exactly what you want—to know everything so you can fix it. There are still many mysteries surrounding autism.

The most important thing to remember through it all is that there is hope. Autism isn't a death sentence. There have been many advancements in the last few years and many children with autism have gone on to lead wonderful, rich lives. So, if you are a parent of an autistic child, do what I do, take a deep breath, dive in, and be the best advocate for your child that you can be.

According to the US Centers for Disease Control and Prevention, one out of every fifty children has an autism spectrum disorder.

And if that's not shocking enough, that statistic doesn't even include adult prevalence or those children who remain undiagnosed—a still too common occurrence.

Children and adults with autism typically experience difficulty with the following:

- Communication, both verbal and nonverbal.

- Making and maintaining consistent eye contact with others.

- Attention span.

- Social skills. Autistic people have a strong propensity toward exclusive activities.

- Routines or repetitive behaviors (i.e., obsessively repeating words or body movements, or arranging belongings in a very specific way).

- Self-help skills, such as toileting, feeding, dressing, brushing teeth, etc.

One person with autism may have very different symptoms and behaviors than another. Because of these differences, doctors think of autism as a "spectrum" disorder, or a group of disorders with a range of similar features. Meaning, a person with mild autistic symptoms is at one end of the spectrum. A person with